THE VIRGINIA SPORTS HALL OF FAME

Honoring Champions of the Commonwealth

VIRGINIA SPORTS MEMORIES. Shown above is a sampling of the ephemera and memorabilia associated with the extraordinary history of sports in the state of Virginia. The trading card featured in the top left corner shows Dave Twardzik of Old Dominion during his days with the Virginia Squires of the American Basketball Association, while the card in the bottom right corner shows Portsmouth native Clarence "Ace" Parker.

THE VIRGINIA SPORTS HALL OF FAME

Honoring Champions of the Commonwealth

Clay Shampoe

ARCADIA

Published by Arcadia Publishing
Charleston SC, Chicago IL, Portsmouth NH, San Francisco CA

Printed in Great Britain

Library of Congress Catalog Card Number: 2004117204

For all general information contact Arcadia Publishing at:
Telephone 843-853-2070
Fax 843-853-0044
E-mail sales@arcadiapublishing.com
For customer service and orders:
Toll-Free 1-888-313-2665

Visit us on the internet at http://www.arcadiapublishing.com

ROANOKE'S FIVE SMART BOYS. In the late 1930s, unheralded Roanoke College fielded a team of basketball players that gained national prominence for their legendary skills on the hardcourt. The young cagers, tagged "The Five Smart Boys," played together all four years of their enrollment, remained unbeaten for three seasons, and captured the state championship from 1937 through 1939. Pictured with Coach "Pop" White, from left to right, are Bob Lieb, Gene Studebacher, Bob Sheffield, White, Johnny Wagner, and Virginia Hall of Fame inductee Paul Rice.

CONTENTS

ACKNOWLEDGMENTS

Many generous and talented individuals supported the completion of this work; therefore, this portion of the book allows me to acknowledge a few of the significant persons who toiled behind the scenes. I would like to personally thank Eddie Webb, executive director for the Virginia Sports Hall of Fame, and his friendly and professional staff, especially Tanya Monton, director of special events and volunteers; Donna Swain, director of administration; and Dan Cawley, director of marketing and sales. Everyone at the Virginia Sports Hall of Fame went above and beyond to assist in the procurement of photos and biographical information for this book. They all made my job much easier and I thank them. Thanks also to my editor at Arcadia, Kathryn Korfonta, for her assistance with the layout of the book.

I would like to bestow special appreciation to my wife of more than 20 years, Deborah, for her continued support and patience as I wrote this book and more importantly, her gift of our time together. Thanks also to my mother, Marion, and brother Jim, as both are continuously supportive in my projects.

I want to lend a rousing cheer of gratitude to my father, Clayton Louis Shampoe Jr., a tough offensive lineman on the 1947 Academy High School football team in his hometown of Erie, Pennsylvania. Through his example, I have learned and experienced the important things in life such as sportsmanship, trust, love, and honor. He was inducted into my personal Hall of Fame years ago.

Clay Shampoe
January 1, 2005

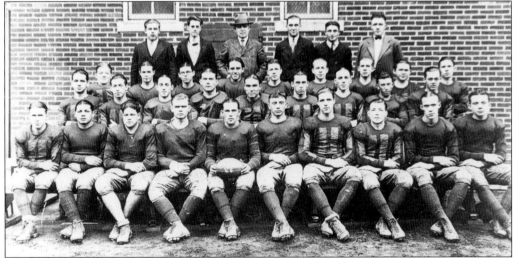

THE "GALLOPING GHOST" AND THE AMAZING 1926 WILSON HIGH PRESIDENTS. Pictured above is Al Casey, Portsmouth's "Galloping Ghost," surrounded by fellow players of the 1926 Wilson High Presidents. From 1926 through 1927, no other team could touch Wilson as they captured back-to-back state championships behind the offensive exploits of Casey. On defense, the Presidents held their opponents scoreless over a remarkable string of 18 straight games.

INTRODUCTION

Hero. Legend. Champion. Superstar. Such is the nomenclature often bantered about to describe the victorious athlete in the arena of sports. Fans often daydream in a Walter Mitty world and fantasize of the home run, touchdown, slam-dunk, or gold medal in the neverland of elite sports. As spectators, fans are relegated to the sidelines, and with good reason, for a champion athlete is a finely tuned entity composed of a unique mixture of coordination, agility, strength, intelligence, and a desire to succeed. To commemorate these special individuals, places of honor have been established that allow us to pay homage to their accomplishments in the world of sports.

In the historic city of Portsmouth, a special shrine has been erected to celebrate the athletic champions of the commonwealth: the Virginia Sports Hall of Fame and Museum. Since its inaugural class was inducted in 1972, the hall has selected more than 225 individuals who have excelled in all fields of sports, as well as reporting, broadcasting, and promoting athletics at an unparalleled level. Whether an inductee was born and raised in the state or came from elsewhere to excel on commonwealth soil, each of these special individuals contributed to the rich sports history of Virginia.

As one explores this book, the reader will immediately notice the marquee names from the world of sports such as Arthur Ashe, Sam Snead, Moses Malone, Willie Lanier, Bruce Smith, and Lawrence Taylor, to name only a few. Beyond the obvious legends found within the context of this book reside many individuals who influenced more than just sports but the nation's social beliefs as well. Many firsts were recorded by Virginians, especially when the color line of athletics was finally broken. William Lewis became the nation's first African American to be named All-American and Virginian Earl Lloyd earned the honorable tag "Basketball's Jackie Robinson" when he became the first African American to play in the National Basketball Association. The competitive sport of auto racing found its color line obliterated by Virginian Wendell Scott, who became a champion on the NASCAR circuit and fought prejudice on and off the track.

The compilation of biographies and photographs found within the pages of this book will never take the place of a personal visit to see the vast collection of memorabilia and artifacts at the hall. Each and every fan of Virginia sports history should set aside a day to experience first-hand the Virginia Sports Hall of Fame and Museum. Use this book as your guide before, during, and after your visit to enhance your journey to this special shrine in the city of Portsmouth.

PHOTOGRAPHY CREDITS
All photographs depicted in this work were used by permission of the Virginia Sports Hall of Fame and Museum and are on file in their offices.

THE ORIGINAL BUILDING HOUSING THE VIRGINIA SPORTS HALL OF FAME. For more than 30 years, the small, red-bricked, Victorian-era building at 420 High Street in Portsmouth housed the Virginia Sports Hall of Fame and Museum. Originally part of the adjoining 1842 courthouse, this unique structure boasted intricate brickwork and high, vaulted ceilings held aloft by massive oak timbers. The building possessed a chapel-like ambience and provided a sanctuary to showcase the vintage memorabilia of the athletes inducted into the shrine. Formerly the office for the Norfolk County Clerk of Courts, the structure became the official home of the Virginia Sports Hall of Fame and Museum in 1977.

ONE

The History of the Virginia Sports Hall of Fame and Museum

With its brick colonnades and cascade of stairs, Portsmouth's courthouse has dominated the corner of High and Court Streets since 1847. This intersection, with sidewalks lined with quaint shops and Victorian-era buildings, serves as the epicenter of historic Olde Towne. Once a neglected jewel within the city, this area is slowly being transformed into a new and exciting urban mecca that municipal leaders continue to polish and buff to accentuate its character. In the past, many buildings in the quarter fell into disrepair as businesses and citizens migrated to the suburbs. For more than a century, a small, chapel-like structure with intricate brickwork rested next to the 1847 courthouse and served as the Norfolk County clerk's office. By 1962, the building stood vacant and neglected. It would be another 15 years before Portsmouth would re-christen the unique structure as the new home for the Virginia Sports Hall of Fame and Museum.

The idea for a Virginia Sports Hall of Fame originated more than a decade before the doors of that small Victorian-era building on High Street officially re-opened. The muse behind the plan was Portsmouth native Herb Simpson. In 1966, as the city's director of emergency services, Simpson was in Dallas, Texas, to attend a law enforcement conference and decided to take a short tour of Dailey Plaza, the site of President John F. Kennedy's assassination. On the way to the plaza, he noticed a building that proclaimed itself as the Texas Sports Hall of Fame. Simpson, a former athlete who played professional baseball in the minor leagues, was intrigued and ventured into the facility. His visit lasted all of 15 minutes, and he left disappointed once he scanned the few photos and uniforms hung about the room to honor the athletes of Texas. From this brief visit, Simpson hatched a plan to create a Virginia Sports Hall of Fame and began a quest to bring his notion to fruition.

As a member of the Portsmouth Sports Club board of directors, Herb Simpson proposed that the group take the initiative to organize a facility to honor the athletes of the commonwealth. With the backing of Portsmouth mayor Richard J. Davis, as well as numerous politicians, businessmen, and sports directors, Simpson's plan was enthusiastically supported. On November 13, 1966, the Virginia Sports Hall of Fame was organized and began to lobby for legislation to name Portsmouth as the site of the shrine. One of the more vocal advocates for a state sports museum was local sports writer Abe Goldblatt, a Portsmouth resident and longtime member of the Norfolk Sports Club. In an article published in the Virginian-Pilot on January 8, 1967, Goldblatt proposed that the Virginia Sports Hall of Fame should be built in the Hampton Roads area and housed in the proposed Norfolk Convention Center, later named Scope. The article listed more than 50 of the most gifted and talented athletes from the commonwealth who should be considered for such a hall.

Goldblatt's proposal to house the memorial in Norfolk surely struck a match under the seats of the Portsmouth group. The publicity strengthened the Portsmouth group's determination and resolve to obtain a legislative order for the hall to be placed in their city posthaste. On February 21, 1968, delegate Glenn Yates submitted Portsmouth's resolution, which passed without conflict through the Virginia Senate and House of Representatives. Fittingly, Herb Simpson was selected to manage the museum as director, and within three years, the Portsmouth group adopted its first by-laws, christened an official seal, and received its articles of incorporation from the state. On December 20, 1971, the Virginia Sports Hall of Fame board of directors selected its first honors court committee to select the inaugural group of inductees.

Still without a building to honor the athletes of Virginia, the honors court selected six legends of the commonwealth as the inaugural group of inductees to enter the Virginia Sports Hall of Fame. During a ceremony in Portsmouth on May 10, 1972, Clarence "Ace" Parker, "Bullet" Bill Dudley, Henry "Cy" Young, Dr. Walter "Whirlwind" Johnson, Bob Spessard, and Eppa Rixey were honored for their sports achievements.

The hall would continue to select six or more new members over the next five years and would include such legends as Sam Snead, Chandler Harper, Bobby Dodd, Henry Jordan, Buster Ramsey, Art Jones, Buzzy Wilkinson, Tommy Thompson, Monk Little, Vic Raschi, Carroll Dale, Joe Weatherly, George McQuinn, Thomas Scott, and Walt Michaels. By the time the 1977 class was inducted, Portsmouth had approved the use of the former clerk's building nestled beside the city's historic courthouse. On April 3, 1977, the Virginia Sports Hall of Fame and Museum opened its doors at 420 High Street followed by an official ribbon-cutting ceremony attended by Gov. Mills Godwin six months later.

The inside of the museum was small with high, vaulted ceilings, ribbed in thick, wooden struts that supported the peaked roof. Simpson designed large plexi-glass showcases to house the large collection of unique memorabilia and placed them throughout the grand exhibit hall of the building. At its opening, the hall displayed more than 35 showcases filled with memorabilia for visitors to view. It would not be long before director Simpson realized that the limited space of the exhibit hall stunted the hall's growth. In just a few years, the hall took over a vacant back room and continued to add new showcases to display the memorabilia of new inductees Bud Metheny, Roosevelt Brown, Arthur Ashe, William Lewis, Buck Noble, Bill Martin, Granny Hamner, George Preas, Deacon Phillippe, Glen Knox, James Gillette, Les Hooker, George Hughes, and Ida Simmons Slack.

After 24 years as executive director and founding father of the Virginia Sports Hall of Fame, Herb Simpson announced that he was ready to step down. Over a storied career in his hometown, Simpson was cited as Portsmouth's Sportsman of the Year twice by the Portsmouth Sports Club and named the city's First Citizen in 1986. He also served a stint on the city council and was a police officer before he was appointed director of Portsmouth's communications and emergency services department. His resignation from the Virginia Sports Hall of Fame took effect July 31, 1995. Shortly after Simpson's announcement, the board of directors selected Virginia Commonwealth University graduate Eddie Webb to assume the leadership of the hall and guide its expansion into the new century.

It wasn't long before the newly appointed director spearheaded a much-needed revival to the hall and convinced city leaders to consider a new location for what many throughout the state felt was the commonwealth's "best-kept secret." In 1996, the immensely popular Children's Museum of Portsmouth drew more than 200,000 visitors a year, while the Virginia Sports Hall of Fame was lucky to attract 40,000 viewers to browse the memorabilia-filled showcases. Director Webb hit the road to promote the hall throughout the state and spent many an evening with small civic groups from Alexandria to Roanoke in his quest to bring more visibility and respectability to the museum.

By the turn of the new century, the city was convinced to include a new building for the sports museum in its innovative refurbishment of the waterfront area and designated a location directly across High Street from the Children's Museum for the future site. At a cost of $11.8 million, the state-of-the-art facility featured a groundbreaking ceremony in 2003, as its construction dominated the High Street corridor of the city. Webb's commitment and dedication to a new Virginia Sports Hall of Fame and Museum was evident in the numbers, as the organization procured more than $8.8 million through fund-raising events and sponsorships.

On September 3, 2004, the original Virginia Sports Hall of Fame building at 420 High Street closed its doors as workers packed away the photos, trophies, and uniforms of the honored inductees of the shrine. Over the winter months, designers organized the new displays in the new 32,000-square-foot museum. There truly is no finer place for fans to enjoy the memorabilia of the most heralded athletes in Virginia sports history. In April 2005, director Eddie Webb and a new class of inductees welcomed the public to the new Virginia Sports Hall of Fame and Museum.

THE HALL'S FOUNDING FATHER AND SPIRITUAL LEADER, HERB SIMPSON. Shown in the exhibit room of the Virginia Sports Hall of Fame in 1980, Herb Simpson leans against the showcase devoted to inductee Arthur "Bud" Metheny. Simpson, a legendary figure in the city of Portsmouth, served as police officer, administrator, and city councilman. He is fondly remembered for realizing his dream of a Virginia Sports Hall of Fame in his hometown of Portsmouth.

DIRECTOR HERB SIMPSON AND 1973 INDUCTEE CHANDLER HARPER. On April 27, 1973, the Virginia Sports Hall of Fame honored its second-year class of inductees. The evening was highlighted by the presentation of the induction plaque from one Portsmouth native to another; here, Herb Simpson welcomes golfer Chandler Harper to the esteemed group of athletes inducted into the shrine.

OFFICIAL VIRGINIA SPORTS HALL OF FAME OPENING. On October 16, 1977, the Virginia Sports Hall of Fame was officially christened with an elaborate ceremony attended by state and local dignitaries, inductees, and the general public. Pictured from left to right are Hall of Famers Julie Conn, Bill Dudley, and Chandler Harper; rounding out the contingent are Gov. Mills Godwin and Lt. Gov. Richard Davis.

THE SHOWCASE OF LEGENDARY TENNIS STAR ARTHUR ASHE. Filled with gleaming silver presentation plates and trophies, the showcase of Richmond native Arthur Ashe was one of the most popular displays at the original Virginia Sports Hall of Fame. Ashe was more than just the most gifted athlete to hail from commonwealth; he parlayed his popularity into beneficial humanitarian and social programs that made significant strides in the progress of race relations and education worldwide.

SHOWCASES OF THE STARS. The original Virginia Sports Hall of Fame featured several rooms displaying the memorabilia of its inductees. In the top right corner are artifacts and photos of Anne Donovan's career, including her Olympic warm-up jacket. At the bottom right is the showcase of Bobby Spangler, a four-sport star at Newport News High and Duke University. Next to the Spangler showcase is that of George Lacy, displaying the equipment used during his career with the Boston Red Sox. In the top left corner, the memorabilia of Virginia Tech gridiron legend Monk Younger is shown.

CINCINNATI REDS LEGENDS VISIT THE HALL. In 1977, Reds announcer Marty Brennaman invited Cincinnati skipper Sparky Anderson for a visit to the hall. As Sparky and their wives admire the memorabilia, Marty (far left) tells the history of fellow Portsmouth native and Wilson High graduate Clarence "Ace" Parker.

CONGRATS FROM THE COACH. Longtime University of Virginia coach Terry Holland (right) makes the formal presentation of the induction plaque to former Cavalier star Ralph Sampson in 1996. The duo led the Charlottesville school to national prominence on the hardcourt during their four years together at UVA. The legendary coach would join Sampson in the Virginia Sports Hall of Fame following his induction in 2003.

PASSING ON A LIFETIME OF WISDOM. At the 1996 induction ceremony, Caroline Sinclair (right) shares some thoughtful insight into her illustrious career in Virginia athletics with fellow Hall of Famer Anne Donovan. Caroline was the oldest living legend to be inducted into the Virginia Sports Hall of Fame when she accepted her plaque in 1996 for her pioneering efforts in women's athletics at Madison College.

DAVE AND THE DIRECTOR. Pictured at the 1999 Legislative Reception at Richmond's old city hall building is Virginia Sports Hall of Fame executive director Eddie Webb (left) and inductee Dave Twardzik (right).

NEW VIRGINIA SPORTS HALL OF FAME'S BUILDING FUND KICK-OFF. Pictured during the kick-off for the new Virginia Sports Hall of Fame are, from left to right, attorney Michael Blachman, inductee Marty Brennaman, Hall of Fame president Bob Aston, and surfing legend Bob Holland. The event for the new Hall of Fame Building Fund was held at a sports restaurant in downtown Portsmouth owned by Roger Brown, a celebrated member of the Virginia Sports Hall of Fame since his induction in 1997.

HALL OF FAMERS HIT THE LINKS. On Saturday, April 24, 2004, Hall of Fame inductees, members, and guests began the 33rd Annual Induction Day with a golf tournament at Portsmouth's Bide-A-Wee Golf Course. Pictured from left to right are (front row) Ace Parker, Buddy Lex, Doris Leigh, and Charlie Moir; (back row) Barry Parkhill, J.R. Wilburn, Kenny Easley, Barty Smith, Walker Gillette, Dell Curry, Chuck Boone, and Paul Webb.

16

CONSTRUCTION OF THE NEW VIRGINIA SPORTS HALL OF FAME. On Wednesday, October 15, 2003, director Eddie Webb and a group of inductees gathered on the corner of High and Middle Streets in Olde Towne to celebrate the beginning of construction for the new Virginia Sports Hall of Fame and Museum. This photo shows the progress in construction in less than 12 months following the ceremonial groundbreaking. The exterior walls of the Hall of Fame showcase the unique brick carvings by local artist Sue Landerman.

THE NEW VIRGINIA SPORTS HALL OF FAME AND MUSEUM. Pictured is an artist's rendering of the front exterior of the new Virginia Sports Hall of Fame and Museum. The 35,000-square-foot building will house interactive exhibits, sports memorabilia, a 125-seat theater, sports activity area, and the Hall of Honor showcasing the accomplishments of Virginia's greatest athletes. The Virginia Sports Hall of Fame and Museum will honor its newest class of inductees on April 23, 2005.

EPPA RIXEY, A VIRGINIA GENTLEMAN. Born in Culpepper on May 3, 1891, Eppa Rixey attended the University of Virginia and excelled in basketball. Standing 6 feet 5 inches tall, he proved to be one of the lankiest players on the squad. The cager was convinced to play baseball by Charlie Rigler, a National League umpire, who served as a coach for the UVA nine. Within three years, the young pitcher made his first major league appearance on June 21, 1912, with the Philadelphia Phillies, never playing a day in the minors. Eppa's best season in pro ball came in 1922 with the Cincinnati Reds, as he posted a record of 25 victories and compiled a 3.53 earned run average over 300 innings. The Culpepper southpaw tallied 266 victories over his major league career and was selected to the National Baseball Hall of Fame in 1963. *Virginia Sports Hall of Fame 1972.*

Two

Legends of the Diamond

As one ponders the accomplishments of the hall's baseball inductees, it is evident that they are as varied and novel as the game itself. Three members honored in the Virginia Sports Hall of Fame also grace the walls at the National Baseball Hall of Fame and Museum in Cooperstown, New York. They are National League pitching legend Eppa Rixey and two players who dominated the Negro Leagues like few others, third baseman Ray Dandridge and hurler Leon Day. While Rixey was one of the esteemed inaugural inductees of the Virginia Sports Hall of Fame, both Dandridge and Day's admission came more than 25 years later. It is interesting to note that Deacon Phillippe, a scrappy, right-handed hurler for the Pittsburgh Pirates and original member of Virginia's Hall of Fame, has not been honored in Cooperstown. Phillippe, a Virginia native and veteran of more than 13 years in the majors, holds the distinct honor of winning what is considered the first World Series game of the modern era, back in 1903.

Many members of the Virginia Sports Hall of Fame enjoyed vibrant and significant careers in the major leagues. Whether they hailed from the urban centers of the commonwealth or the farmlands, Virginia baseball players excelled on the diamond. Henrico County's Hermitage High School produced one of baseball's most consistent shortstops, Gene Alley of the Pittsburgh Pirates, while rural Farnham, Virginia, claims New York Yankee pitcher Jim Coates as a native son. Many fans wonder what heights Richmond's Mel Roach might have attained in the majors had he not suffered a horrendous injury on the diamond with the Milwaukee Braves in 1958.

Several of the hall's inductees can claim to be a special part of baseball lore. Few realize that Norfolk's Bud Metheny was the last New York Yankee to wear Babe Ruth's uniform number before it was officially retired by the team or that two Granby High athletes, Chuck Stobbs and Hank Foiles, were football stars in the inaugural Oyster Bowl game in 1946. Stobbs holds the distinction of serving up Mickey Mantle's historic tape measure home run at Griffith Stadium, while Foiles, a longtime veteran of pro ball, became the first major league catcher to wear contact lenses during play.

Others with major league time on the diamond include Granny Hamner, Vic Raschi, Al Bumbry, George McQuinn, Williard Marshall, Lefty Vaughn, Bob Porterfield, and Clyde McCullough. Several Virginia ballplayers, such as Johnny Oates and Jim Lemon, made a name for themselves as major leaguers and then enjoyed successful careers as coaches and managers in the game. Exceptional careers on the diamond at the state level were attained by Randolph-Macon skipper Hugh Stephens and University of Richmond manager Mac Pitt, as well as players George Lacy, Rosie Thomas, Lefty Wilson, and Taylor Sanford. The business and administrative part of the game is covered with the induction of longtime major league baseball man Syd Thrift and minor league executive Frank D. Lawrence.

All of the inductees honored in the Virginia Sports Hall of Fame for their contributions to the game proved to be special and gifted individuals who made an impact on the history of baseball.

PIRATES SHORTSTOP, GENE ALLEY. Born in Virginia's Henrico County, Leonard Eugene Alley proved to be a natural on the diamond as he honed his skills at Hermitage High School. Making his major league debut with the Pirates as a 22-year-old shortstop in 1963, Gene soon became a fixture in the Pittsburgh infield for 11 solid seasons. In 1966, he batted an impressive .299 from the plate while gathering 173 hits. The Richmond native earned a spot on the National League All-Star roster in 1966 and 1967 and added a Gold Glove to his trophy case each of these years as well. *Virginia Sports Hall of Fame 1989.*

PORTSMOUTH'S "MR. BASEBALL," FRANK D. LAWRENCE. Frank Dudley Lawrence (center) was considered "Mr. Baseball" in his hometown of Portsmouth for more than half a century. A self-made banker, Lawrence was nicknamed "The Battler" for his innovative methods to keep his independently owned minor league team, the Portsmouth Cubs, competitive against his major league–backed opponents. In 1943, he was honored by *The Sporting News* as Minor League Executive of the Year. *Virginia Sports Hall of Fame 1985.*

BASEBALL'S FIRST WORLD SERIES HERO, DEACON PHILLIPPE. Born in Rural Retreat, Virginia, on May 23, 1872, Charles Louis Phillippi (Phillippe) began his baseball career as a 27-year-old pitcher for Louisville of the National League. During his first major league season, he proved to be an immediate success, amassing an impressive record of 21 victories. The following season, he found himself in Pittsburgh pitching for the Pirates and remained their workhorse on the mound for 12 seasons, finishing out his career in 1911. In an era of many great pitchers, Deacon proved to be one of the best as he accumulated 189 wins against only 109 losses. His control on the mound was superb as he led the National League in issuing the fewest walks per game for five out of six years running. In 1903, in what is considered the first official World Series of the modern era, Deacon took the mound as the opening game pitcher for the Pirates against the American League Boston Pilgrims; he led his team to a 7 to 3 victory over the home team and their pitcher, Cy Young. While Pittsburgh eventually lost the series, Deacon led the Bucs with three victories and a low 2.86 ERA. *Virginia Sports Hall of Fame 1982.*

PITCHER JIM COATES. Born in Farnham, Virginia, on August 4, 1932, James Alton Coates pitched in his first professional game while still a teenager and later signed a contract with the New York Yankees in 1951. As "Big Jim" worked his way through the minors, he spent time with the Norfolk Tars and later the Richmond Virginians. The lanky hurler made his major league debut in 1956 but suffered a mishap on the diamond the following season in which he broke his pitching arm, thus putting his career in jeopardy. It took the Virginia native two more years before he regained his major league form, pitching effectively for the Yankees through the 1962 season. *Virginia Sports Hall of Fame 1994.*

SKIPPER HUGH STEPHENS. A native of Staunton, Hugh Stephens attended Randolph-Macon College and excelled on both the hardcourt and the diamond. As the baseball team's ace hurler, he compiled an impressive record of 20-9 over his four years at the college. Hugh began his coaching career immediately after graduation at the prep level and returned to his alma mater in 1949, serving as the school's athletic director and basketball coach. In 1950, he began an impressive 32-year run as the baseball coach for Randolph-Macon as he guided his players to 31 winning seasons and 10 small college state championships. *Virginia Sports Hall of Fame 1994.*

SOUTHPAW CHUCK STOBBS. A multi-talented sports star at Norfolk's Granby High, Chuck Stobbs was named the Virginia Player of the Year for 1946 for his accomplishments in football, basketball, and baseball. After graduation, the 17-year-old West Virginia native signed a contract with the Boston Red Sox and found himself pitching in Fenway Park before his first professional season came to an end. For the next 14 seasons, Chuck toiled on the mound for a number of major league teams, winning 107 games over a storied pro career. The Norfolk native will be forever immortalized for serving up the pitch that Mickey Mantle rocketed out of Griffith Stadium on April 17, 1953. The tape measure home run traveled 565 feet before finally returning to earth. *Virginia Sports Hall of Fame 2002.*

BASEBALL GURU JOHNNY OATES. From his early days on the diamond at Prince George High School and later Virginia Tech, Johnny Oates proved he was one of the best receivers to man the plate. Drafted after only two years out of college by the Baltimore Orioles in 1967, Johnny would go on to play in the majors with a number of National and American League teams. After 11 baseball seasons catching a baseball, he began a second career in the game as a leader from the dugout. Following a short stint in the minors, Johnny served as coach with the Cubs and the Orioles before taking over for Frank Robinson as Baltimore's new skipper. His finest years at the helm came with the Texas Rangers as he led the team to three American League Western Division pennants. *Virginia Sports Hall of Fame 2003.*

ARTHUR "BUD" METHENY. Born on June 1, 1915, in St. Louis, Arthur Beauregard Metheny began his pro ball career in the New York Yankees minor league system and played for the 1938 Norfolk Tars along with Phil Rizzuto. By 1943, Bud earned a spot with the Yankees and served as an outfielder during the war years. While baseball was his first love, Bud knew the value of a college education; he graduated from William and Mary and continued to play in the minors, appearing with the Portsmouth Cubs and Newport News Dodgers while away from his studies. Bud served as athletic director at Old Dominion University from 1963 until 1970 and skippered numerous baseball and basketball teams. In 1965, Bud was honored as NCAA baseball Coach of the Year. *Virginia Sports Hall of Fame 1979.*

AL BUMBRY, ROOKIE OF THE YEAR. Alonza Benjamin Bumbry, a native of Fredericksburg, proved to be an inspiration to many on both the diamond and the battlefield. The fleet-footed outfielder spent 13 of his 14 major league seasons with the Baltimore Orioles, capturing the American League Rookie of the Year Award in 1973 with a .337 batting average. One of only a handful of major league ballplayers who served in Vietnam, Al was awarded a Bronze Star for meritorious service in the conflict overseas. Upon returning stateside, he became an integral part of Baltimore's success during the 1970s and early 1980s and is proud to wear a World Series ring from the 1983 fall classic when the Orioles topped the Phillies in five games. In 1980, Al put together a banner year, batting an impressive .318 and collecting 205 hits. He was among the league leaders in stolen bases (44) and runs scored (118). *Virginia Sports Hall of Fame 2002.*

BASEBALL HALL OF FAMER RAY DANDRIDGE. When considering all the exceptional baseball players who patrolled third base on the diamond, there was no one better than Ray Dandridge. A native of Richmond, the small-framed and bow-legged infielder was one of the brightest stars in the Negro National League before the integration of baseball at the major league level. Ray brilliantly served for the Newark Eagles for seven seasons with additional time spent in the Mexican League and Cuban Winter League. Once the color line was broken in 1947 and blacks were allowed to play alongside their white counterparts, Ray was signed by the New York Giants and placed on the roster of their minor league affiliate Minneapolis, where he batted .318 and won the American Association Most Valuable Player Award in 1950 at the age of 37. In 1987, Ray Dandridge was named to the National Baseball Hall of Fame in Cooperstown, New York. *Virginia Sports Hall of Fame 1999.*

VIC RASCHI, THE SPRINGFIELD RIFLE. Hailing from Springfield, Massachusetts, Victor Angelo Raschi first enrolled at William and Mary College in 1938 and starred for the Tribe's baseball team as a freshman. He signed with the New York Yankee organization in 1941 and pitched for their Class B Piedmont League team, the Norfolk Tars, in 1942. After spending three years in the Army Air Corps during the war, Vic returned to toil in the minors before finally earning a spot in the Yankee rotation in 1946. Once "The Rifle" settled into the big leagues, he was almost unstoppable and turned in three consecutive seasons of 21 victories from 1949 through 1951. Overall, his career stats in the majors are impressive, with 132 victories against only 66 losses, yielding a .667 winning percentage. *Virginia Sports Hall of Fame 1976.*

MEL ROACH, A CAREER CUT SHORT. In the late 1940s, Mel Roach was a talented athlete at Richmond's John Marshall High where he was named All-City on the hardcourt and All-Southern in football and baseball. Following two years at UVA, Mel signed with Milwaukee and dethroned Red Schoendienst to become the starting second baseman for the Braves. In 1958, with 44 games under his belt, Mel was batting an impressive .309 as rumors circulated that he was a lock for National League Rookie of the Year. On August 3, during a routine double play, Mel was involved in a collision at second base that severely tore ligaments in his left knee. Following extensive rehab, Mel returned to the game but played only briefly before his premature retirement. *Virginia Sports Hall of Fame 1988.*

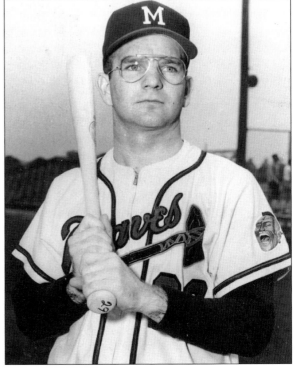

PHILLIES WHIZ KID "GRANNY" HAMNER. Born in Richmond, Virginia, on April 26, 1927, Granville Wilbur Hamner began a 14-year major league career in 1944 with the Philadelphia Phillies. An agile shortstop with sure hands, Granny led the National League in at bats with 662 in 1949 and was a member of the famed Philadelphia "Whiz Kids" of 1950. Despite the fact that the 1950 Phillies were swept in the World Series by the New York Yankees, Granny batted an impressive .429 in a losing cause. Following the 1959 season, he began to play as well as manage in the minor league system and was the first skipper for the Tidewater Tides during their inaugural season in Portsmouth in 1961. Granny was enticed to return to the majors in 1962 by the Kansas City Athletics but not in his usual position as shortstop. Instead, he found himself on the mound pitching three games in relief for the American League team. *Virginia Sports Hall of Fame 1981.*

ALL-STAR GEORGE McQUINN.
This Arlington, Virginia native
made his major league debut with
the Cincinnati Reds on April 14,
1936. George later proved to be
one of the premier first basemen
in the American League as a
member of the St. Louis Browns
from 1938 through 1945. In his
first season with the Browns, he
batted .324 and put together an
impressive 34-game hitting streak.
George was selected to the
American League All-Star team
six times over a 12-year major
league career and accumulated
1,588 hits, 135 home runs, and a
solid .276 batting average. The
Virginia native completed his
playing days with the New York
Yankees in 1948. *Virginia Sports
Hall of Fame 1978.*

WILLARD MARSHALL. This Richmond
native honed his baseball skills on the
diamond of Manchester High School and
played part-time with a number of local
American Legion teams as a teenager.
Following a year of study at Wake Forest,
Willard left school and signed his first pro
contract with the New York Giants of the
National League. The unheralded rookie so
impressed Giant manager Mel Ott that the
Hall of Famer penciled the novice outfielder
into his starting lineup on opening day
1942. Following a three-year tour of duty
with the Marines during World War II,
Willard returned to the Giants in 1946 and
put together an impressive season the
following year as he hit 36 home runs and
batted .291 from the plate. The Virginia
native was selected to the National League
All-Star team in his rookie year (1942) and
recaptured the honor again in 1947 and
1949. *Virginia Sports Hall of Fame 1990.*

NEGRO LEAGUE LEGEND LEON DAY. Born in Alexandria on October 30, 1916, Leon Day was a true triple threat on the baseball diamond, consistently besting his opponents with his fine pitching, impeccable defensive skills, and dynamic hitting. The Virginia native will be remembered as the ace of the Newark Eagles of the Negro National League in the late 1930s and 1940s; his best season was in 1937 when he tallied an unblemished 13-0 record in league play and batted .320 from the plate. His playing career spanned from 1934 until 1949, and he appeared in a record seven East-West All-Star games over ten campaigns in the Negro Leagues while playing additional seasons in Puerto Rico, Cuba, Venezuela, Mexico, and Canada. On a memorable summer day in July 1942, Leon struck out 18 Baltimore Elite Giant batters for a Negro League record. While never allowed the opportunity to play integrated ball at the major league level, Leon's accomplishments in the game earned him a well-deserved plaque at the National Baseball Hall of Fame in Cooperstown in 1995. *Virginia Sports Hall of Fame 2002.*

SPIDER SKIPPER "MAC" PITT. Malcolm "Mac" Pitt began his long association with the University of Richmond as a freshman in 1915 where he quarterbacked the football squad and anchored the hot corner on the diamond for the Richmond nine. Following graduation, he began an illustrious coaching career at Fork Union Military Academy before returning to his alma mater in 1928 as an assistant football coach. Mac's greatest accomplishments came as skipper for the UR baseball team as he guided the Spiders to a 426-257 record over 37 seasons, winning the state championship 16 times. *Virginia Sports Hall of Fame 1974.*

PIRATE CATCHER HANK FOILES. Born in Richmond in 1929, Henry Lee "Hank" Foiles Jr. and his family moved to Norfolk where he earned multiple letters in football, baseball, and track at Granby High. In 1946, Hank was named All-Southern in football and starred in the inaugural Oyster Bowl game held at Norfolk's Foreman Field. While numerous colleges were offering scholarships for the Granby star to play on the gridiron, Hank opted for a baseball career and signed with the New York Yankees. For 11 seasons, he served on a number of major league teams including Cleveland, Baltimore, and finally Pittsburgh. While with the Pirates as their starting catcher in the late 1950s, Hank enjoyed his finest years in the majors, earning a spot on the National League All-Star squad in 1957. *Virginia Sports Hall of Fame 1987.*

BIG JIM LEMON, THE "COVINGTON CRUSHER." From 1950 until 1963, Jim Lemon made a name for himself in the American League while displaying impressive numbers as a member of the Cleveland Indians, Washington Senators, Minnesota Twins, Philadelphia Phillies, and the Chicago White Sox. A native of Covington, Virginia, the 6-foot 4-inch slugger's 12-year major league career yielded 164 home runs. Big Jim's most spectacular season came in 1950 when he was among the league leaders as he bashed 38 home runs and 100 RBIs for the Senators. Following his playing days, he took on the role of coach and manager for a number of teams and returned to skipper the Senators in 1968. Jim's most memorable night came in 1956 with the Yankees visiting Griffith Stadium. With ace Whitey Ford on the mound, the Covington Crusher sent three consecutive home runs over the wall during the contest. *Virginia Sports Hall of Fame 1988.*

ALL-STAR BOB PORTERFIELD. Born in Newport, Virginia, in 1923, Erwin Cooledge "Bob" Porterfield first displayed his knack for pitching a baseball past opposing batters as a hurler for the Norfolk Tars, where he notched 17 victories during the 1947 campaign. The righthander made his major league debut in 1948 with the New York Yankees but was traded to Washington during the 1951 season. In 1953, Bob had a stellar year as he led the American League with 22 wins while posting 9 shutouts for the lowly Senators. *Virginia Sports Hall of Fame 2005.*

SOUTHPAW "LEFTY" VAUGHN. Born in Stevensville, Cecil Porter Vaughan boasted an impressive collegiate career on the diamond for the University of Richmond Spiders. The talented hurler led the team to a state championship in 1940 as he pitched a record six shutouts during the season and led the Southern Conference with fewest hits allowed and most strikeouts tallied. On April 21, 1940, Lefty made his major league debut with the Philadelphia Athletics and spent two seasons with the team, returning for a single game in 1946 following service in the air force. *Virginia Sports Hall of Fame 1993.*

VIRGINIA SPORTS HALL OF FAME NOTABLES
Additional "Legends of the Diamond" Inductees

♦ **SYD THRIFT.** Considered by many to be one of the most influential men in baseball, Syd Thrift first established his love for the game on the diamond at Randolph-Macon College, where he earned All-State honors. He tasted the life of the pro ballplayer for only a short time before an injury prematurely ended his playing days. Baseball was fortunate to have Syd continue to contribute to the sport as one of the game's most successful and knowledgeable executives. Over his career, he has worked in the front offices of the Oakland Athletics, the New York Yankees, the Chicago Cubs, and the Baltimore Orioles. During the 1980s, he virtually rebuilt the lowly Pittsburgh Pirates into one of baseball's most successful franchises and was named major league baseball's General Manager of the Year in 1988. *Virginia Sports Hall of Fame 1998.*

♦ **CLYDE MCCULLOUGH.** A native of Nashville, Tennessee, Clyde Edward McCullough began playing the game of baseball at the age of 17 as an infielder with a local American Legion team. He signed his first pro contact the following year and began to work his way through the New York Yankee minor league system until the team sold him to the Chicago Cubs in 1940. Known for his powerful physique and toughness behind the plate, Clyde would at times catch without a chest protector. Mostly used as a platoon player with the Cubs, Clyde had a major league career spanning 15 years. Following his playing days, Clyde served as manager, coach, and scout for a number of major and minor league teams. In 1969, he led the Tidewater Tides to the International League pennant. *Virginia Sports Hall of Fame 1983.*

♦ **GEORGE LACY.** A multi-talented athlete at the University of Richmond, George lettered in football, basketball, and baseball with the Spiders. His talents were evident on the diamond as George served as the team's star catcher during his four years at Richmond, earning All-State honors three times. After graduation, he signed with the Boston Red Sox organization and enjoyed several successful minor league seasons before signing on as a scout with the Twins. *Virginia Sports Hall of Fame 1996.*

♦ **CHARLES "ROSIE" THOMAS.** A native of Buckingham County, Virginia, Rosie Thomas became a legend coaching football, baseball, and basketball at Fork Union Military Academy beginning in 1930. His accomplishments include 6 state titles in football and basketball and 14 in baseball. *Virginia Sports Hall of Fame 1993.*

♦ **LAWRENCE "LEFTY" WILSON.** Lefty Wilson is considered to be one of UNC's greatest pitchers as he posted 40 victories over four seasons during the 1920s. As a pro ballplayer, Lefty played minor league ball and later enjoyed a stellar coaching career at Danville's George Washington High School. Over his 40 years at the school, he captured five state championships. *Virginia Sports Hall of Fame 1986.*

♦ **TAYLOR SANFORD.** One of the most heralded athletes in the history of the University of Richmond, Taylor Sanford earned 13 letters in football, basketball, baseball, and track. Following graduation, Taylor served as a distinguished coach at Hargrave Military Academy, Randolph-Macon, and, later, Wake Forest, where he was named NCAA National Baseball Coach of the Year. *Virginia Sports Hall of Fame 1977.*

BILL DUDLEY, THE BLUEFIELD BULLET. Hailing from Bluefield, Virginia, "Bullet" Bill Dudley did not play his first football game until his senior year at Graham High School. He quickly proved his worth on the gridiron and excelled as a halfback and place kicker before accepting a scholarship to attend the University of Virginia. As a Cavalier, Bill earned All-American status in 1941 and set a national scoring record with 134 points as UVA boasted an impressive 8-1-0 record. Following graduation, Pittsburgh selected him as the No. 1 pick in the 1942 NFL draft, and the Bluefield Bullet captured Rookie of the Year honors with the Steelers in his inaugural pro season. During a pro career that spanned nine seasons, Bill suited up for the Steelers, Lions, and Redskins and developed into one of the best offensive players in the history of the National Football League. In 1966, Bill Dudley was inducted into the Pro Football Hall of Fame. *Virginia Sports Hall of Fame 1972.*

THREE

Greats of the Gridiron

Virginia is often referred to in history books as the "State of Presidents" for the profusion of citizens from the commonwealth to be elected the nation's leader. Despite this lofty title, many fans believe the old adage should be amended to proclaim that Virginia is the "State of Gridiron Greats" for its knack to produce some of the nation's greatest football stars. When one looks over the list of inductees that grace the walls of the Virginia Sports Hall of Fame, it is understandable why the old saying should be challenged, for Virginia has produced some the best players to ever run, pass, tackle, and kick the pigskin during the past century. Currently, the Pro Football Hall of Fame in Canton, Ohio, can boast of more than a few Virginia legends, including Clarence "Ace" Parker, "Bullet" Bill Dudley, Dwight Stephenson, George Allen, Roosevelt Brown, Willie Lanier, Lawrence Taylor, Henry Jordan, and Lou Creekmur. It is only a matter of time before Bruce Smith, a member of Virginia's Hall of Fame Class of 2005, will heed the call to Canton as well.

Legendary teams and players will forever be a part of Virginia's football legacy. Few can forget the amazing streak put together by Charlottesville's Lane High as they tallied 53 straight victories during the 1960s under the guidance of the "Golden Greek," Tommy Theodose. Another legendary moment in the history of football in the commonwealth occurred when Norfolk's Granby High School football squad of 1945 scored an incredible 440 points over 10 games as they captured the state title with an unblemished record. Countless other special teams and individual accomplishments will be remembered as a part of the commonwealth's rich gridiron history.

At the collegiate level, such legends as Bill Dudley, Buck Mayer, and John Papit brought national recognition to the University of Virginia Cavaliers, while Hunter Carpenter, Frank Loria, and Bruce Smith are part of the lore that helped establish Virginia Tech as a national powerhouse. The casual football fan may be surprised to learn that Washington and Lee, which began intercollegiate play on the gridiron in 1873, was once a nationally ranked team to be reckoned with, while William and Mary produced some of pro football's most recognized players, including Henry Jordan of Vince Lombardi's Green Bay Packers.

The historic rivalry between the University of Virginia and Virginia Tech is always a hot topic of conversation any time of the year but comes to a head as the fall chill envelops Lane Stadium in Blacksburg and the mountains surrounding Charlottesville. Now that Virginia Tech has joined UVA in the Atlantic Coast Conference, the rivalry has only escalated to new heights of passion and exuberance.

While no NFL team has taken up residence in the commonwealth, professional football once enticed thousands of fans to fill stadiums throughout the state. In Hampton Roads, fans of the Norfolk Neptunes crammed Foreman Field on the campus of Old Dominion University during the late 1960s and early 1970s as the Continental Football League flourished in a number of cities across the nation. The Neptunes proved to be a solid football team with a huge and faithful fan base that supported the team until its demise by the mid-1970s. Since then, semi-pro teams throughout the commonwealth have supplied fans with games on a limited basis.

On the following pages, the reader will discover the greats of the gridiron that made names for themselves playing the game of football. Some will be familiar while others may be more obscure but are surely worthy in their achievements of the game itself. No matter, each inductee featured is a true champion, one that the commonwealth of Virginia is proud to call its own.

EARL FAISON, ROOKIE OF THE YEAR. Born in Newport News, William Earl Faison became a multi-talented sports star at Huntington High. By his senior year, Earl had matured into a massive 6-foot 5-inch, 265-pound defensive end. He continued his education at Indiana University where he was named All-American as a senior in 1960. The following year, he was signed by the San Diego Chargers of the American Football League and was named Rookie of the Year. Over his six years as a professional on the gridiron, Earl was named to the All-Pro team in 1961, 1963, and 1964. *Virginia Sports Hall of Fame 1989.*

BOBBY DODD. Born in Galax in 1908, Bobby Dodd grew up in Tennessee and honed his skills on the gridiron in Kingsport. The multi-talented athlete excelled at the University of Tennessee and earned nine letters in football, baseball, basketball, and track. Bobby took his first coaching position as an assistant under Bill Alexander at Georgia Tech in 1931. He formally stepped into Alexander's shoes in 1945 and brought Tech to national prominence over the next 22 years. With Bobby at the helm, the school attended 13 post-season bowl games and won 9. His 1952 team finished the year unbeaten and ranked No. 2 in the nation. *Virginia Sports Hall of Fame 1973.*

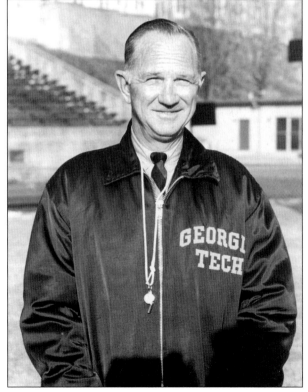

PORTSMOUTH'S OWN, CLARENCE "ACE" PARKER. Born and raised in Portsmouth, Clarence Parker left Churchland High in 1930 when the school decided to field a football team no longer. The following year, the Virginia native was convinced to enroll at neighboring Woodrow Wilson High and developed into one of the best high school athletes in the commonwealth. At Duke University, he was christened "Ace" and crowned All-American in 1936 for his play on the gridiron. With the stage set for a promising football career, Ace opted to sign with the Philadelphia Athletics and hit a home run in his first major league at bat. It took some convincing by the NFL Brooklyn Dodgers to motivate Ace to turn in his bat and sign a contract to play football. Over the next five seasons, he led the hapless Dodgers to a new level of respectability and was named the National Football League's MVP in 1940. In 1972, Ace was inducted into the Pro Football Hall of Fame. *Virginia Sports Hall of Fame 1972.*

GEORGE ALLEN, CHIEF OF THE REDSKINS. In 1948, George Allen assumed his first coaching position at Morningside College, and by 1966, his expertise and work ethic earned him a spot as a National Football League head coach with the Los Angeles Rams. George later served as the guiding force in the resurgence of the Washington Redskins for seven seasons as he compiled an impressive record of 67-30-1. *Virginia Sports Hall of Fame 1998.*

TRIBE CAPTAIN MARVIN BASS. A native of Petersburg, big Marv Bass captained one of William and Mary's most successful gridiron teams in history during the 1942 season. The Tribe posted a record of 9-1-1 and bested the Oklahoma Sooners 14-7 on the final game of the campaign to make it a season to remember. That same year, Marv was named to the All-State and All-Southern Conference squads. Following graduation, he pursued a lengthy and successful coaching career with a variety of collegiate and professional football teams. *Virginia Sports Hall of Fame 1981.*

FULLBACK JACK "FLYING" CLOUD. An Okie native raised in Norfolk, Jack Cloud made a name for himself on the gridiron at Maury High School in the early 1930s. Following a stint in the military during World War II, Jack enrolled at William and Mary and guided the Tribe to some of the best football ever witnessed in the school's history. His ability to run rampant with the pigskin earned him All-American status in 1947 and 1948. Jack's professional career spanned four seasons but was cut short by injuries. He returned to William and Mary to coach, followed by an assignment as athletic director at the Norfolk Naval Station. His success in Norfolk led to a position at the Naval Academy, where he served as a staff coach for the Plebes over a 22-year period. *Virginia Sports Hall of Fame 1984.*

ALL-PRO WALT MICHAELS. Born in Pennsylvania, Walt Michaels proved to be one of the most dominating players in Washington and Lee's football history. In 1951, Walt led the Generals to their first post-season bid and an appearance in Jacksonville's Gator Bowl. After graduation, Walt began a pro career with the Green Bay Packers in 1951, followed by 10 seasons with the Cleveland Browns. During his Lake Erie tenure, he earned All-Pro honors four times as the NFL's top linebacker and was a vital cog in Cleveland's five division titles and two world championships. In 1962, Walt began an NFL coaching career with the Oakland Raiders and was later named head coach of the New York Jets in 1976. *Virginia Sports Hall of Fame 1977.*

JIMMY LEECH, KING OF THE KEYDETS. Born in Lexington, James C. "Jimmy" Leech attended Virginia Military Institute from 1916 through 1920 and became the school's first bona fide All-American in football. During his final year as a Keydet, Jimmy scored an amazing 210 points, leading an undefeated VMI squad to victories over such powerhouses as North Carolina, Penn, Virginia, Virginia Tech, and NC State. Virginia Military virtually crushed their opponents, scoring a total of 431 points compared to only 20 for their challengers over the entire 1920 season. During his time at VMI, he also excelled at baseball, basketball, track, tennis, swimming, and golf. For his many accomplishments in athletics, Jimmy Leech was named to the National College Football Hall of Fame. *Virginia Sports Hall of Fame 1973.*

COACH BOBBY ROSS. Robert Joseph Ross was born in Richmond on December 23, 1936, and became a three-sport letterman at Virginia Military Institute. The Virginia native was assigned his first college head-coaching job with the Citadel in 1973 and continued to make a name for himself at the University of Maryland as he led the Terrapins to three ACC titles and four post-season bowl appearances. In 1990, Bobby led the Georgia Tech Yellow Jackets to a share of the national championship. This successful collegiate skipper then served as head coach with the San Diego Chargers and Detroit Lions from 1992 through 2000, for an NFL career that spanned nine seasons. In December 2003, Bobby came out of retirement and accepted the head coaching position at West Point. *Virginia Sports Hall of Fame 1997.*

ROOSEVELT BROWN, A GIANT IN THE NFL. In his first year at Charlottesville's Jefferson High, Roosevelt "Rosey" Brown Jr. was snatched from the school band and convinced to play for the football team. Forbidden to play the sport following the death of his older brother on the gridiron, Rosey suited up without his father's knowledge. With his mother serving as mediator, Rosey played an impressive, injury-free year, and his father became his biggest fan. Following graduation, Rosey entered Morgan State and won Black All-American honors all four years. His skills drew only limited attention from the New York Giants, and he was drafted deep in the 27th round. With little expected of such an insignificant selection, Rosey surprised his coaches and earned a starting position his rookie year. From 1956 until 1963, there was no one better on the offensive line as he captured numerous All-NFL honors and guided the Giants to six division championships and one NFL title. Rosey was named NFL Lineman of the Year in 1956 and started every game of his pro football career with the exception of three. For his accomplishments on the gridiron, Roosevelt Brown was inducted into the Pro Football Hall of Fame in 1975. *Virginia Sports Hall of Fame 1979.*

CAVALIER WILLIAM THOMAS.
William Talley Thomas was born in Richmond and began his football career on the gridiron of McGuire Prep School. There, he won All-City honors in football, baseball, and track and was named to the Virginia All-State football squad. William entered the University of Virginia in 1928 and over a four-year period was named Collegiate All-State three times and All-Southern once and earned All-American Honorable Mention in 1930. William turned down a number of pro offers and opted to remain at UVA as an assistant coach while continuing his education. *Virginia Sports Hall of Fame 1985.*

ALL-PRO LARRY BROOKS.
Lawrence Lee Brooks, a native of Prince George, earned All-Central District honors as a defensive end in 1967 as a high school senior. Larry enrolled at Virginia State and was chosen Little All-American, Virginia State College Lineman of the Year, and All-Conference. During his 11 seasons with the Los Angeles Rams, Larry was named to the Pro Bowl five straight seasons and was an All-Pro selection three times. Following his career on the defensive line, the Virginia native transitioned to coaching with the Rams. Later, he was named defensive line coach for the Green Bay Packers and was instrumental in guiding the team to a Super Bowl championship. *Virginia Sports Hall of Fame 2000.*

NFL ALL-STAR KEN WILLARD.
Born in Richmond on July 14,
1943, Kenneth Henderson
Willard was awarded 16 varsity
letters during his prep years at
Varina High School. The
heralded athlete enrolled at the
University of North Carolina and
earned a spot on the 1964 All-
ACC team in both baseball and
football. That same year, Ken was
named All-American by *Parade*
magazine and the College
Coaches Association. While
playing for the San Francisco
49ers, Ken was elected to the
NFL All-Pro team three times
and finished his pro career with
over 6,200 yards gained and more
than 60 touchdowns scored.
Virginia Sports Hall of Fame 1985.

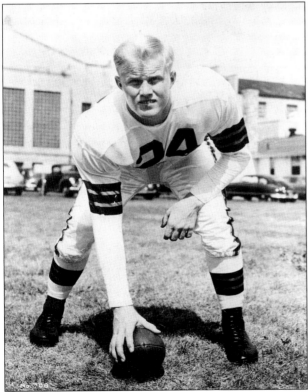

CENTER TOMMY THOMPSON.
Considered by many to be one of
the greatest lineman in the history
of William and Mary football,
Tommy Thompson was the rock of
the Tribe front line in the late
1940s. As a collegiate, Tommy
earned All-State honors as center
for three consecutive seasons from
1946 to 1948 and was named All-
American in his senior year. A
solid pro career commenced in
1949 with Cleveland and spanned
five seasons until his retirement in
1953. During that time, Tommy
was named All-Pro twice and
served as team captain for the
Browns. *Virginia Sports Hall of
Fame 1975.*

STEVE DELONG. Born in Chesapeake on July 3, 1943, Steve DeLong was the defensive star for Oscar Smith High, where he was named All-State and All-American in 1960. Steve entered the University of Tennessee and continued his fine defensive work for the Volunteers from 1962 through 1964. His list of honors includes the Outland Trophy, awarded to the nation's top lineman, as well as All-American status in 1963 and 1964. Steve spent eight years in the pro ranks with the majority of his time as a San Diego Charger, where he earned a Pro Bowl selection. Steve DeLong was named to the National College Football Hall of Fame in 1993 and was selected to the All-Time Tennessee team in 1990. *Virginia Sports Hall of Fame 2000.*

WILLIAM BEATTIE FEATHERS. Born on August 4, 1908, Beattie Feathers began his football career at Virginia High in his hometown of Bristol where he earned All-State honors. Considered by many to be one of the commonwealth's most talented gridiron men, Beattie became a legend at the University of Tennessee for his running and kicking skills and was named All-American as a Volunteer. At Tennessee, he scored 32 touchdowns in only 30 games from 1931 to 1933 and amassed 1,888 rushing yards, a record that lasted 47 years before it was broken. Beattie spent seven seasons in the National Football League and set a pro record by averaging 9.9 yards per carry in his rookie year with the Chicago Bears. Following his playing days, Beattie served as head football coach at both Appalachian State and North Carolina State. *Virginia Sports Hall of Fame 1981.*

THE WONDER FROM WISE, CARROLL DALE. During his four years on the gridiron at Virginia Tech, Carroll Dale became the Hokies' first bona fide All-American and displayed a unique talent to snag a football on the fly and score touchdowns. Following graduation, Carroll entered the NFL with the Los Angeles Rams and later served as the premier pass catcher for Vince Lombardi's legendary Green Bay Packers from 1965 until 1972. *Virginia Sports Hall of Fame 1976.*

WILLIAM FULLER, THE SACK MAN. Born in Norfolk and raised in Chesapeake, William Fuller excelled in both football and track at Indian River High School. Playing for the University of North Carolina, William developed into one of the best defensive linemen in the nation and was honored with All-American status for two consecutive seasons. The Virginia native began his pro career with the Philadelphia Stars of the United States Football League and led the team to back-to-back championships before the league folded. Picked up immediately by the Houston Oilers, William was selected to his first Pro Bowl in 1991 and was honored three more times as a member of the Philadelphia Eagles. *Virginia Sports Hall of Fame 2004.*

CAVALIER JOE PALUMBO. Considered by many to be one of the best defensive guards in University of Virginia football history, Joe Palumbo was the foundation of the Cavalier varsity line from 1949 through 1951. The Pennsylvania native earned All-American honors in 1951 and was named Virginia's Athlete of the Year for his exploits on the gridiron. Joe was drafted by the San Francisco 49ers following graduation, but he opted for a military uniform rather than an NFL jersey and served with honor in Korea. In 1999, Joe Palumbo was inducted into the National Football Foundation's Hall of Fame. *Virginia Sports Hall of Fame 1973.*

JOLTIN' JOE MUHA. Born in Central City, Pennsylvania, Joe Muha developed into one of the most celebrated and talented football players ever to grace the gridiron at the Virginia Military Institute. Tagged with the moniker "Joltin' Joe," the 6-foot, 200-pound running back was named All-State and All-American and finished second as National Player of the Year in 1942. Upon graduation, Joe served in the U.S. Marines during World War II and was awarded the Presidential Unit Citation for his heroics on the battlefield. Upon his return stateside, Joe began a five-year pro career with the Philadelphia Eagles where he was named All-NFL in 1947, 1949, and 1950. *Virginia Sports Hall of Fame 1976.*

CAVALIER ALL-AMERICAN AND NFL ROOKIE OF THE YEAR TOMMY SCOTT. Thomas Coster Scott, a native of Baltimore, is considered one of the all-time gridiron greats in University of Virginia history. Always referred to as Tommy, the talented Cavalier played both offensive and defensive end and was named All-American in 1952. Upon graduation, he was signed by the Philadelphia Eagles and captured Rookie of the Year honors in the NFL. In 12 pro seasons, he was named All-Pro seven times and appeared in four Pro Bowl games. Following his playing days, Tommy Scott served as a respected defensive coach with the New York Giants. *Virginia Sports Hall of Fame 1997.*

RECEIVER J.R. WILBURN. Born in San Diego in 1943, Johnnie Richard Wilburn was raised in Portsmouth, Virginia, and began his football career at Cradock High. His skills as a sure-handed receiver earned him a scholarship to the University of South Carolina, where he developed into a remarkable, two-sport collegiate star. On the gridiron, J.R. earned All-American status and was named to the All-State football squad twice. As a track star, he excelled in the javelin toss, the triple jump, and the high jump. Upon graduation, he signed with the Pittsburgh Steelers and enjoyed a solid five-year NFL career. *Virginia Sports Hall of Fame 2004.*

CAVALIER HALFBACK BUCK MAYER. A native of Norfolk, Buck Mayer attended the University of Virginia in pursuit of a law degree and found success on the gridiron for the Cavaliers from 1912 through 1915. Buck set a number of records in Charlottesville, including points scored in a single game (36), most touchdowns in a season (21 in 1914), most career touchdowns (48), and career points scored (312). Besides football, Buck excelled in track and specialized in the shot put, broad jump, and 100-yard dash. This talented Virginian is considered the South's first All-American as recognized by Walter Camp in 1915. *Virginia Sports Hall of Fame 1980.*

THE SEATTLE STREAK, KENNY EASLEY. A standout at Chesapeake's Oscar Smith High, Kenny Easley earned numerous gridiron honors, including All-Southeastern District, All-Tidewater, All-South, and All-American from 1973 through 1977. Considered to be one of the best athletes to come out of Hampton Roads, Kenny attended UCLA and was named a three-time All-American and All-PAC-10 during his four years in Los Angeles. In 1981, the Seattle Seahawks made Kenny their first round draft pick, and over a seven-year pro career, the Virginia native was selected to the Pro Bowl five times and named the NFL's Defensive Player of the Year. *Virginia Sports Hall of Fame 1998.*

NFL LINEBACKER ED BEARD. Edward Leroy Beard was born in Chesapeake on December 9, 1939, and starred on the gridiron at Oscar Smith High. After graduation, Ed enrolled at the University of Tennessee and was named All-State, All-Conference, and All-American with the Volunteers before joining the army. With his enlistment completed, the Hampton Roads native began a solid National Football League career as a linebacker with San Francisco and served as team captain for the 49ers specialty unit. Following 8 solid years as a pro, Ed opted to remain with the league and logged 10 seasons as a respected NFL coach. *Virginia Sports Hall of Fame 2002.*

ALL-AMERICAN AL NEMETZ. Born in Prince George in 1922, Albert "Al" Nemetz starred on the Hopewell High School football squad and later enrolled at Wake Forest University. The Virginia native transferred to West Point and began an illustrious collegiate career with the Black Knights, where he was named consensus All-American in 1945. Following his graduation from the military academy, Al served his country in two wars and enjoyed a long and honorable military career. *Virginia Sports Hall of Fame 1986.*

HALL OF FAME LINEMAN LOU CREEKMUR. Lou Creekmur was named All-Southern and All-American in 1949 as a tough offensive lineman at William and Mary. The Tribe star was signed by the Detroit Lions and quickly earned a starting role on the team's front line. Over the next ten seasons, Lou was named to the Pro Bowl eight years and was an All-NFL selection six times. A true gridiron machine, Lou played in 150 straight games until his retirement following the 1958 season. When approached in the early weeks of the 1959 season by the Lions to return for another year, Lou quickly put on the pads and resumed his role as a starting offensive lineman. During his long tenure with the Lions, Lou led the team to three NFL championships and entered the Pro Football Hall of Fame in 1996. *Virginia Sports Hall of Fame 1989.*

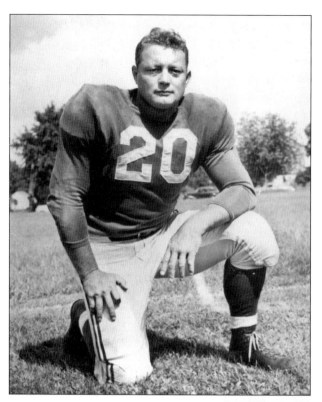

TRIBE GUARD BUSTER RAMSEY. Born and raised in Tennessee, Garrard "Buster" Ramsey excelled on the gridiron of Knoxville High and was named All-Southern and All-Tennessee guard in his senior year. Buster entered William and Mary and was selected All-Southern for three years and All-American in 1942. Pro football beckoned, and the Tribe guard signed with the Chicago Cardinals, where he was named All-Pro three times. Following his playing days, the Tennessee native began an illustrious coaching career with the Detroit Lions as a defensive coach and later served as Buffalo's first head coach. *Virginia Sports Hall of Fame 1974.*

WILLIAM H. LEWIS, THE NATION'S FIRST BLACK ALL-AMERICAN. Born in Norfolk in 1868, William H. Lewis served as captain of the Amherst College football squad. The young African American was accepted into Harvard Law School in 1892 and was named the first All-American of his race to excel on the gridiron. Despite his slight build and weight, William excelled as a defensive lineman when not studying for the bar. Following his Ivy League years, he continued to serve the school as a line coach and later authored a helpful guide to future gridiron stars titled "How to Play Football." In 1911, with a Harvard degree in hand, William became the first African-American to be admitted to the American Bar Association and was appointed assistant attorney general under President Howard Taft. *Virginia Sports Hall of Fame 1980.*

THE LORD OF LOMBARDI'S LINE, HENRY JORDAN. Born in Emporia in 1935, Henry excelled in football, track, and wrestling at Warwick High School in Newport News, where he was named All-Tidewater and All-State Honorable Mention. He entered the University of Virginia in 1953 and was named All-State and All-ACC for his work on the Cavalier gridiron line. Henry's pro career began with the Cleveland Browns until he was traded to the Green Bay Packers in 1959, where he served under Coach Vince Lombardi as part of football's most historic dynasties. Over the next 11 seasons, Henry started for the Packers as defensive tackle and earned All-NFL honors 6 times. For his accomplishments on the gridiron, Henry Jordan was inducted into the Pro Football Hall of Fame in 1995. *Virginia Sports Hall of Fame 1974.*

FLEET-FOOTED LEROY KEYES. Born and raised in Newport News, Leroy Keyes was a triple threat at Carver High, excelling at football, basketball, and track. As a Boilermaker at Purdue University, the Virginia native set a number of rushing records and led the nation in points scored over the season (122). From his halfback position, he did it all and even threw for 8 touchdowns and completed 12 of 22 passes. Leroy earned consensus All-American status in his final two years at Purdue and finished second to O.J. Simpson for the 1968 Heisman Trophy. When the NFL beckoned, the fleet-footed Keyes was selected in the first round by the Philadelphia Eagles and remained with the team until he was traded to the Kansas City Chiefs. His NFL career spanned five years but was cut short by a leg injury. *Virginia Sports Hall of Fame 1987.*

ALL-AMERICAN ERIC TIPTON. A native of Petersburg, Eric Tipton led the Duke Blue Devils to an astounding 25 victories against only 4 defeats during his varsity tenure and was named All-American in 1938. Rather than donning the pads for an NFL career, Eric signed on with Connie Mack's Philadelphia Athletics in 1939. Used sparingly by the Athletics over three seasons, he was traded to the Cincinnati Reds and became an integral part of the 1944 team when he batted an impressive .301 from the plate. Following his career in the majors, Eric served as baseball coach at West Point for many years before his retirement. *Virginia Sports Hall of Fame 1978.*

NFL STAR SONNY RANDLE. Ulmo Shannon "Sonny" Randle excelled in football, basketball, and track at Fork Union Academy and continued his legacy at the University of Virginia, where he was named All-American. In 1959, Sonny signed with the Chicago Cardinals and spent ten years in the NFL with a variety of teams, including the San Francisco 49ers and the Dallas Cowboys. During the 1960s, no one was better at catching a pass as he snagged more pigskins for touchdowns than anyone else in the league. During his NFL career, he was selected to the Pro Bowl four times and was named All-Pro three consecutive seasons. Following his playing days, Sonny served as head football coach at East Carolina, UVA, and Marshall. He is credited with mentoring baseball Hall of Fame speedster Lou Brock in his base running skills. *Virginia Sports Hall of Fame 1991.*

JIM GILLETTE, THE COURTLAND COURIER. A native of Courtland, Jim Gillette began his football career at the University of Virginia as a "walk-on" player who quickly proved his worth on the gridiron. He earned All-State honors as a daring, broken-field runner and defensive specialist. His potential was noted by the Cleveland Browns, who signed the "Courtland Courier" to a contract for the 1940 NFL season. Following a stint in the military, Jim resumed his role with the Browns for two seasons and eventually suited up with the Boston Yanks, Green Bay Packers, and Detroit Lions before his retirement from pro football in 1948. The gridiron bloodlines passed down to Jim's son, Walker, an NFL veteran and fellow Hall of Fame inductee. *Virginia Sports Hall of Fame 1983.*

SURE-HANDED WALKER GILLETTE. Born in Norfolk on March 16, 1947, Walker Adams Gillette attended the University of Richmond and earned All-American status for his sure hands and speed on the gridiron. One of the all-time great Spiders, Walker set a number of school passing records and was named Southern Conference Player of the Year in 1969. The Virginia native was selected in the first round of the NFL draft and his pro career spanned seven years as he donned the uniforms of the San Diego Chargers, St. Louis Cardinals, and New York Giants. A speedster with reliable hands, Walker averaged over 15 yards per catch and pulled in more than 150 passes during a solid NFL career. *Virginia Sports Hall of Fame 1990.*

NFL Hall of Famer Willie "Contact" Lanier. Willie Edward Lanier was born on August 21, 1945, in Clover, Virginia, and began a stellar football career at Maggie Walker High School. Willie chose to attend Morgan State University for a degree in business and was accepted to the school more on his scholastic merits than his excellence on the gridiron. At Morgan State, he developed into a small college All-American linebacker and was awarded his degree in business administration in 1967. Willie, a second-round NFL draft choice of Kansas City, remained with the Chiefs throughout an impressive 11-year pro career. From 1967 to 1977, no one in the NFL was better at bringing down an elusive runner than Willie Lanier. He earned All-Pro honors eight seasons, appeared in six Pro Bowl games, and was named NFL "Man of the Year" in 1972. Willie Lanier was elected to the Pro Football Hall of Fame in 1986. *Virginia Sports Hall of Fame 1986.*

SPIDER LEGEND ED MERRICK.
University of Richmond fans remember Ed Merrick as one of the most talented athletes to ever play for the Spiders. For three straight seasons, from 1938 to 1940, Ed was voted the outstanding tackle in the commonwealth and was named All-Southern during that span. After serving with honor in World War II, Ed returned to his alma mater as the UR head football coach and was named Southern Conference Coach of the Year twice. *Virginia Sports Hall of Fame 1980.*

NFL LINEMAN GEORGE PREAS.
Born in Richmond and raised in Roanoke, George Preas developed into a talented athlete at Jefferson High, where he earned prep honors in football and wrestling. At Virginia Tech, George proved instrumental in the transformation of the Hokies from doormats into one of the best teams in the nation. The Virginia native was named All-American, All-State, and All-Conference during his tenure at Tech. George's pro career spanned 11 years as a valued lineman with the Baltimore Colts from 1955 until his retirement following the 1965 NFL season. *Virginia Sports Hall of Fame 1982.*

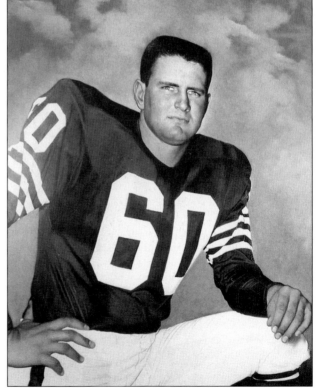

IRONMAN DWIGHT STEPHENSON. Dwight Stephenson began his football career at Hampton High as a defensive end and was selected to the All-State Group AAA team in 1975. His role changed upon enrollment at the University of Alabama, where he assumed the position of center and earned All-American status. Dwight's pro career spanned eight years, all with the Miami Dolphins, and included five NFL Pro Bowl appearances. The "Dolphin Ironman" played in 107 consecutive games from 1980 until the players' strike in 1987. Unfortunately, a serious knee injury in 1988 cut his NFL career short. For his leadership, superb blocking, and excellence handling of a football, Dwight Stephenson was inducted into the Pro Football Hall of Fame in 1998. *Virginia Sports Hall of Fame 1999.*

HUNTER CARPENTER.
Considered to be "the greatest gobbler of them all," Hunter Carpenter began his football career at Virginia Tech using the alias Walter Brown to hide his participation on the gridiron from his father. Born in 1883 in Clifton Forge, Hunter starred as a speedy halfback and kicking specialist at VPI from 1900 to 1903. In an unusual move, he left Tech and played the 1904 season with the University of North Carolina before returning to Blacksburg in 1905 to captain the Hokie team to one of the best seasons in the school's long gridiron history. *Virginia Sports Hall of Fame 1973.*

LYNN CHEWNING. Born in Columbia, South Carolina, Lynn Chewning's family moved to Richmond in 1931. While attending high school in the commonwealth's capital, Lynn won All-City honors for his exploits on the gridiron. In 1947, he transferred to Hampden-Sydney and excelled in football and track and won All-State honors in both sports and Little All-American status on the gridiron. Following his collegiate career, Lynn played professionally with the New York Bulldogs in 1949 and the Richmond Rebels in 1950. *Virginia Sports Hall of Fame 1991.*

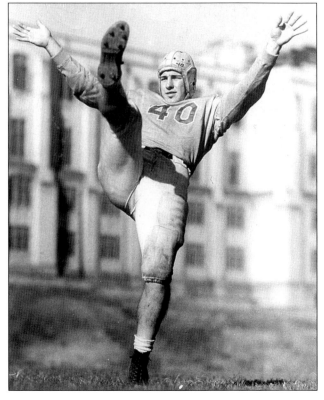

NORM SNEAD, THE WARWICK WARRIOR. Born in Halifax County on July 31, 1939, Norman Bailey Snead honed his skills as a multi-talented athlete at Warwick High School in Newport News. At Wake Forest, he set numerous single game and career passing records that stood unsurpassed for more than two decades. Following graduation, Norm was drafted by the Washington Redskins, threw 11 touchdowns his rookie year, and doubled his total the following season. His lengthy career in the National Football League spanned 16 seasons as quarterback for the Philadelphia Eagles, Minnesota Vikings, New York Giants, and San Francisco 49ers. Over his pro career, Norm passed for more than 30,000 yards, threw 196 touchdown passes, and appeared in the NFL Pro Bowl three times. Upon his retirement, Norm coached ten seasons at the shipyard in Newport News for the Apprentice School. *Virginia Sports Hall of Fame 1984.*

BOSH PRITCHARD. Born in Windsor, North Carolina, in 1919, Abisha "Bosh" Pritchard was noted for his great open field running as a Virginia Military Institute Keydet from 1938 to 1942. At VMI, Bosh lettered in football, track, baseball, and basketball. The ever-exuberant Bosh was also a respected crooner for the school's dance band and was often heard singing a melody during practice sessions on the gridiron. His NFL career spanned six years, and the VMI legend led the league in rushing average for the 1949 season. *Virginia Sports Hall of Fame 1977.*

GREEN BAY PACKER BARTY SMITH. Barton Elliot "Barty" Smith was selected as Virginia's High School Player of the Year and Sunkist All-American in 1969 for his excellence on the gridiron at Douglas Freeman High in Richmond. Barty opted to continue his education at the University of Richmond and led the Spiders to a Tangerine Bowl appearance and a top-20 Division I ranking in the nation. He spent his entire seven-year NFL career with the Packers and was named Green Bay Offensive Player of the Year in 1977. *Virginia Sports Hall of Fame 1999.*

ROGER BROWN, ALL-PRO DEFENSIVE TACKLE. Roger Lee Brown was born on May 1, 1937, and was raised in Newport News as a child. By the time Roger completed his collegiate career at Maryland State, he topped the scales at 298 pounds and stood a towering 6 feet 5 inches tall. He earned a reputation as a fierce competitor on the gridiron and was named NAIA All-American in 1959. Signed by the Detroit Lions in 1960, Roger finished second in the NFL Rookie of the Year balloting after an impressive inaugural season. Along with teammate Alex Karras and the rest of the Lions' defensive line, Roger became an integral part of the original "Fearsome Foursome" and was selected to the NFL Pro Bowl five consecutive seasons. Traded to the Los Angeles Rams in 1967, Roger joined Deacon Jones, Merlin Olsen, and Lamar Lundy as the new Fearsome Foursome was reborn on the West Coast. Without missing a beat, Roger again was selected to his sixth Pro Bowl and completed a remarkable ten-year NFL career in 1969. *Virginia Sports Hall of Fame 1997.*

IRONMAN GEORGE HUGHES. Born and raised in Norfolk, George Hughes excelled on the gridiron at Maury High as both center and linebacker for the Commodores. After his enlistment during World War II, the Virginia native enrolled at William and Mary and earned All-State and All-Conference gridiron honors in 1949. From 1950 until 1954, George was the cog of the Pittsburgh Steelers offensive line and was named to the NFL All-Pro squad in 1952 and 1954. Following his pro career, he retired to Norfolk but returned to the game in 1965 to coach the Norfolk Neptunes of the Continental Football League. *Virginia Sports Hall of Fame 1983.*

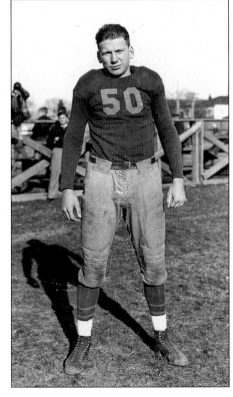

SUFFOLK SPEEDSTER ART JONES. Raised in Hampton Roads, Art Jones attended Suffolk High and excelled in football, track, tennis, and basketball. In the late 1930s, he led the University of Richmond Spiders on the gridiron and was named All-State three years in a row. During a Southern Conference track meet, Art was timed at 10 seconds in the 100 meters and proved that few were faster. He was a first round draft choice of the Pittsburgh Steelers and earned All-Pro honors his rookie season. The "Suffolk Speedster" is immortalized as the first player in the NFL to discard the traditional high-topped shoes in exchange for the less restrictive low profile style, now a mainstay in the pro game. *Virginia Sports Hall of Fame 1975.*

64

ONE OF THE GREATEST ON THE GRIDIRON, LAWRENCE TAYLOR. Born in Williamsburg on February 4, 1959, Lawrence Taylor is unquestionably one of the greatest linebackers in the history of the game. The Virginia native began his remarkable football career at Lafayette High and continued to shine at the University of North Carolina, earning All-American honors on the Chapel Hill gridiron. Lawrence, who was named NFL Rookie of the Year in 1980 and Player of the Year in 1986, appeared in 13 Pro Bowl games as a New York Giant. Known for his ferocious play on the field and his ability to suit up and excel while injured, Lawrence Taylor is among the NFL leaders in many defensive categories. For his monumental accomplishments on the gridiron, "LT." was named to the Pro Football Hall of Fame in 1999. *Virginia Sports Hall of Fame 2003.*

SPIDER DICK HUMBERT. Born in Pennsylvania and raised in Suffolk, Dick Humbert went on to gridiron fame at the University of Richmond. As a pro with Philadelphia, he was named the league's Rookie of Year and later led the Eagles to consecutive NFL championships in 1948 and 1949. Upon retirement from the game, Dick returned to the University of Richmond and served as the chairman of the physical education department for more than 20 years. *Virginia Sports Hall of Fame 1981.*

BUDDY LEX, THE TRIBE'S TRIPLE-THREAT TAILBACK. Born in Norfolk, Joseph "Buddy" Lex excelled in multiple sports at Newport News High, where he earned All-State honors in football and basketball. Buddy enlisted in the army after graduation and participated in the Battle of the Bulge. Upon his return stateside, Buddy enrolled at William and Mary and became one of the most feared triple-threat tailbacks to operate from the single wing. In 1949, the Norfolk native led the nation in touchdown passes completed and was ranked among the top collegiate players in passes completed and punting yardage. *Virginia Sports Hall of Fame 1986.*

BRUCE SMITH, THE NFL's "SECRETARY OF DEFENSE." In the history of the NFL, there was no one better at stalking and sacking opposing quarterbacks than Bruce Smith. Born in Norfolk, Bruce excelled on the gridiron at Booker T. Washington High School and continued his dominance on the defensive line with the Virginia Tech Hokies. While at Tech, he was named All-American twice and awarded the prestigious Outland Trophy. In 1985, Bruce was the No. 1 pick in the NFL draft and began an illustrious 15-year career with the Buffalo Bills. He made 11 Pro Bowl game appearances and led the Bills to four consecutive Super Bowls. On December 7, 2003, Bruce set a new NFL record with his 199th career sack. Over an amazing NFL career, this Virginia native played in 279 games and was credited with 908 tackles and 200 sacks. *Virginia Sports Hall of Fame 2005.*

J. STOCKLEY FULTON. A talented center on the Hampden-Sydney College gridiron squad, J. Stockley Fulton was named Little All-American in 1954 and was awarded the prestigious Gammon Cup. The gifted athlete returned to his alma mater and coached Hampden-Sydney to national prominence in 1976 with a top-five Division III ranking. *Virginia Sports Hall of Fame 1977.*

"POUNDING PAUL" SHU. Paul Shu was a gifted, multi-star athlete at George Washington High in Alexandria before his enrollment at Virginia Military Institute. Nicknamed "Pounding Paul" for his style of play on the gridiron, the speedy Keydet was the first athlete in VMI history to letter in four sports. In 1937 and 1938, Paul was selected First-team All-Southern Conference, but an injury the following season forced him to become an effective blocker instead of a dangerous running back. Paul is shown posed with the winning game ball from the November 23, 1939 contest against arch rival Virginia Tech. *Virginia Sports Hall of Fame 1983.*

VIRGINIA SPORTS HALL OF FAME NOTABLES
Additional "Greats of the Gridiron" Inductees

- MELVIN "MEB" DAVIS. This noted athlete began his football career at Maury High and Norfolk Collegiate and excelled on the gridiron at William and Mary from 1924 to 1927. Meb returned to his alma mater to coach the Tribe and later skippered the Richmond Arrows of the Dixie Professional League. *Virginia Sports Hall of Fame 1984.*

- ROLAND DAY. A legend at Petersburg High, Roland Day led his gridiron squad to an impressive record of 114-24 during a career that spanned from 1932 to 1945. *Virginia Sports Hall of Fame 1979.*

- JAMES "SUEY" EASON. Born in 1907, this South Norfolk native developed into an outstanding athlete at William and Mary and excelled in football and baseball. Suey made a name for himself as coach at Hampton High from 1940 through 1960, as he led the Crabbers to a remarkable 158-50-14 record and three state championships. *Virginia Sports Hall of Fame 1990.*

- KARL "DICK" ESLEECK. One of the all-time great coaches in the history of the Virginia High School League, Dick led three different prep teams to the state championship over his career: Hampton High in 1936, John Marshall in 1940 and 1941, and Portsmouth's Woodrow Wilson in 1947. *Virginia Sports Hall of Fame 1977.*

- DICK FLETCHER. Fresh from college, Dick Fletcher signed on as football coach at Norfolk's Maury High School as a 21-year-old novice. Despite his young age and lack of experience, his leadership abilities soon became evident as he led the Commodores to the state football championship in 1932 and 1935. *Virginia Sports Hall of Fame 1989.*

- WILLIAM "PEDIE" JACKSON. A multi-talented athlete at Emory and Henry College, Pedie returned to his alma mater and became a legend at the small school when he led the team to national recognition on the gridiron with a 9-0 record in 1927. Over his coaching career, Pedie guided Emory and Henry to a remarkable 62-13-4 record as the offense amassed 1,378 points while their opponents could muster only a mere 348. *Virginia Sports Hall of Fame 1979.*

- THAD MADDEN. A graduate of Virginia State, Thad Madden developed into one of the most successful coaches in the commonwealth. While at the helm, he led Huntington High of Newport News to 16 Eastern District titles and 7 state championships. *Virginia Sports Hall of Fame 1988.*

- LEE McLAUGHLIN. An All-State selection in football at Richmond's John Marshall High, Lee McLaughlin later starred on the gridiron at the University of Virginia. He began an illustrious football-coaching career after one year of pro ball and guided Washington and Lee to an undefeated season as they were named national small college champion. *Virginia Sports Hall of Fame 1987.*

VIRGINIA SPORTS HALL OF FAME NOTABLES
Additional "Greats of the Gridiron" Inductees

- ◆ **FRANK SUMMERS.** A gifted athlete and student, Frank Summers excelled at Virginia Military Institute at football, baseball, basketball, and track. The Alexandria native played tackle for VMI's "Flying Squadron," the institute's only undefeated, untied football team. *Virginia Sports Hall of Fame 1975.*

- ◆ **JOHN TODD.** A four-sport star at the College of William and Mary from 1921 to 1925, John Todd served as team captain for the Tribe and was considered one of the best centers to ever play on the school's gridiron squad. *Virginia Sports Hall of Fame 1978.*

- ◆ **MONK YOUNGER.** A football legend at Davidson and Virginia Tech, Monk Younger was labeled the "Southern Panther" in 1916 for his skill on the gridiron by renowned football analyst Walter Camp. Born in Danville and raised in Lynchburg, Monk later served as a respected coach, first at Davidson and later Virginia Tech. *Virginia Sports Hall of Fame 1977.*

- ◆ **FRANK PEAKE.** A football star at Hampton High and All-American at Virginia Tech, Frank Peake was an integral part of the school's famous "Pony Express" backfield from 1925 to 1928. *Virginia Sports Hall of Fame 1978.*

- ◆ **SONNY WADE.** Born in Martinsville, Sonny Wade was named Virginia's College Player of the Year in 1966, 1967, and 1968 while enrolled at Emory and Henry College. His pro career was spent in Canada as he quarterbacked the Montreal Alouettes to the CFL Grey Cup three times. *Virginia Sports Hall of Fame 1994.*

- ◆ **MAC MCEVER.** This legendary football leader began his gridiron career with Virginia Tech in 1925 and later became a successful and respected coach at the University of North Carolina. *Virginia Sports Hall of Fame 1980.*

- ◆ **CHARLES PERDUE.** One of the famed "Iron Dukes" on the 1938 Duke University gridiron squad, Charles "Bolo" Perdue was an All-State halfback with the Blue Devils and named to a number of All-American teams. Bolo played briefly in the NFL with the New York Giants and the Brooklyn Dodgers. *Virginia Sports Hall of Fame 1993.*

- ◆ **AL CASEY.** A native of Portsmouth, Virginia, Al Casey was nicknamed the "Galloping Ghost" at Virginia Tech for his broken field running on the gridiron. As a member of the Wilson High squad (see page 6), Al and the Presidents captured the state football championship in 1926 and 1927. *Virginia Sports Hall of Fame 1982.*

- ◆ **CARTER "NELLIE" CATLETT.** Born in Norfolk, this multi-talented Virginian excelled in football, basketball, and track at Hampton High and later Virginia Military Institute. *Virginia Sports Hall of Fame 1994.*

- ◆ **BOBBY SPANGLER.** A four-sport star at Newport News High School, Bobby starred on the gridiron at Duke University as a talented center, end, and running back. *Virginia Sports Hall of Fame 1992.*

VIRGINIA SPORTS HALL OF FAME NOTABLES
Additional "Greats of the Gridiron" Inductees

♦ **RALPH CUMMINS.** One of the winningest coaches in the history of Virginia, Ralph led Clintwood High to 271 victories over his 40-year career. His honors include National High School Coach of the Year in 1987. *Virginia Sports Hall of Fame 1996.*

♦ **OTIS DOUGLAS.** This unheralded student-athlete at William and Mary developed into a superb football player with little or no experience when he first suited up for the Indians. At the relatively old age of 35, Otis played in his inaugural NFL game with the Philadelphia Eagles and later served as their trainer for four years. He later coached the Baltimore Colts and provided consulting services to the Cincinnati Reds. *Virginia Sport Hall of Fame 1979.*

♦ **VITO RAGAZZO.** A football legend at William and Mary, Vito held a number of NCAA gridiron records with the Tribe as a pass receiver and scorer. The West Virginia native played professionally in Canada with the Hamilton Tiger-Cats and led his team to the Grey Cup title in 1953. He served on the sidelines as a coach with VMI, East Carolina, Wake Forest, and Shippensburg State and also scouted for the New England Patriots of the National Football League. Among his many accomplishments, Vito was named College Coach of the Year in 1981 and 1982. *Virginia Sports Hall of Fame 1993.*

♦ **GEORGE "GUMMY" PROCTOR.** Born in Fredericksburg in 1907, George "Gummy" Proctor officiated his first basketball game at the age of 15. He served as a successful athletic coach at Virginia Tech and later Washington and Lee. Once he returned to officiating, this Virginia native enjoyed a long and successful career as a college referee. *Virginia Sports Hal of Fame 1974.*

♦ **BILL MERNER.** A legendary coach at Hopewell High, Bill Merner led the Blue Devils to an impressive record of 74-25-1 over his career. Under Bill's leadership, Hopewell was an offensive powerhouse and totaled 26,560 points during his tenure. The stadium at Hopewell High was dedicated as Merner Field out of respect for their legendary coach. *Virginia Sports Hall of Fame 1990.*

♦ **THOMAS L. SCOTT.** A prep star at Norfolk's Maury High, Thomas was named All-State, All-Conference, and All-American at Virginia Military Institute. He served as the inaugural coach at the Norfolk Division of the College of William and Mary from 1930 to 1941. *Virginia Sports Hall of Fame 1989.*

♦ **FRANK LORIA.** Virginia Tech's first consensus All-American, Frank earned this honor in 1965 and 1966 as a defensive safety. After graduation, Frank became an offensive coordinator at Marshall University and tragically died in a plane crash with the rest of the gridiron squad in 1970. *Virginia Sports Hall of Fame 1984.*

THE PRIDE OF PETERSBURG, MOSES MALONE. As a cager at Petersburg High, there was no prep player as dominant on the hardcourt as Moses Malone. By graduation, the 6-foot 10-inch center drew the attention of every college in the nation as he led Petersburg to an incredible 50-game winning streak and back-to-back state championships. During his inaugural season as a professional, Moses was named to the American Basketball Association's All-Rookie team and was chosen to play in the annual All-Star game. When the ABA folded, Moses began an impressive 19-year NBA career and was named to the All-Star team 12 times, honored as league MVP 3 times, and led the Philadelphia 76ers to a championship in 1983. On October 5, 2001, "The Pride of Petersburg" was officially inducted into the National Basketball Hall of Fame. *Virginia Sports Hall of Fame 1999.*

FOUR

Heroes of the Hardcourt

Virginia has a rich history of collegiate basketball as many schools throughout the commonwealth have gained national prominence over the years. NCAA championships and Final Four appearances are part of the legacy at the University of Virginia, Virginia Tech, Old Dominion, Virginia Commonwealth, and the University of Richmond. The wealth of talent that has come out of these and other schools throughout the state has produced such legendary players as Anne Donovan, Allen Bristow, Buzzy Wilkerson, Bob Spessard, Dell Curry, Barry Parkhill, Glen Knox, Nancy Lieberman, Bobby Dandridge, Dave Twardzik, Les Hooker, Bob Kilbourne, and Glenn Robert, to name only a few.

As one can see from the notables listed above, the state has bred basketball stars from both the men's and women's programs. It has been within the past quarter century that women's hoops at the collegiate level has gained almost as much popularity as when the men take the court. In Virginia, the Lady Monarchs of Old Dominion University have been at the forefront of this new wave of popularity. The ball-handling skills of Nancy Lieberman and Anne Donovan brought national recognition to the commonwealth at Norfolk's Old Dominion University.

Two of Virginia's most famous native sons earned elite status on the basketball court and achieved their accomplishments by very different roads to a similar end. Petersburg's terrific teenager, Moses Malone, proved to be one of the most talented cagers in the nation and took the road less traveled directly to professional basketball, while Harrisonburg's Ralph Sampson honed his skills at the University of Virginia before entering the pro ranks. Both achieved success in each of their venues as Sampson dominated college ball for four years and Malone took the American Basketball Association and later the National Basketball Association by storm.

While Virginia is renowned for its strong collegiate basketball teams, the commonwealth had a taste of the big time during the 1970s as part of the American Basketball Association. The Virginia Squires became the first professional basketball franchise to operate in the state of Virginia and played "home" games in Hampton, Norfolk, Richmond, and Roanoke. The team roster was peppered with phenomenal and legendary players such as Charlie Scott, Larry Brown, Doug Moe, Julius "Dr. J" Erving, and George "The Iceman" Gervin. In a move to fill the arenas scattered throughout the state, owner Earl Foreman signed ODU guard Dave Twardzik and UVA's Barry Parkhill to play for the Squires. While the franchise suffered financially, the Squires provided basketball fans throughout the commonwealth with an exciting brand of play characteristic of the American Basketball Association. The Squires were fortunate to hang on until the final days of the ABA in 1976 but were not invited to join New York, San Antonio, Indiana, and Denver in the merger with the National Basketball Association at the end of the season.

Some of the other legends of basketball who grace the walls at the Virginia Sports Hall of Fame include Glen Roberts, Buzzy Wilkerson, and Earl Lloyd, the first African-American to play in the National Basketball Association. The mentors of the sideline are represented by such coaching legends as Lefty Driesell, Julie Conn, Charlie Moir, Jimmie Bryan, Terry Holland, "Rasty" Doran, and Paul Webb. Each inductee featured within this chapter has a myriad of accomplishments on the hardcourt that has earned them a special place in the Virginia Sports Hall of Fame and Museum.

ALL-AMERICAN BOB SPESSARD. Born in Roanoke on December 11, 1915, Robert Woods "Bob" Spessard led the Jefferson High cagers to the 1934 Class A State Championship. In 1935, Bob entered Washington and Lee, was named All-State for three consecutive years from 1935 to 1937, and was honored as a Helms All-American in his senior year. The multi-talented athlete also excelled on the gridiron and was elected to the state All-Star squad for his exploits in football. *Virginia Sports Hall of Fame 1972.*

CAVALIER BUZZY WILKINSON. A legend on the hardcourt at the University of Virginia, Buzzy Wilkinson led the nation in scoring (32.1 points per game average), earned All-American status, and was named Athlete of the Year in the State of Virginia in 1955. This Cavalier cager was a torrid scorer and tallied 2,233 points over his career at UVA. Following graduation, he was drafted by the Boston Celtics of the National Basketball Association but never had the opportunity to play, since injuries suffered in a car accident terminated his pro career before he ever started. Buzzy returned to UVA to coach and completed his law degree in 1962 following a tour of duty in the military. *Virginia Sports Hall of Fame 1975.*

NATIONAL BASKETBALL HALL OF FAMER ANNE DONOVAN. Following an impressive high school career in New Jersey, Anne Donovan selected Old Dominion University as her home court from 1979 to 1983. During that span, Anne was named a three-time All-American and was selected the Naismith Player of the Year in her final year at ODU. With Anne controlling the backboards and fellow Hall of Famer Nancy Lieberman directing the backcourt, the Lady Monarchs captured the AIAW National Championship in 1979. Once away from ODU, Anne played pro ball for seven seasons and was a three-time Olympian with two gold medals to her credit. After six years as an assistant coach at ODU, she accepted her first head coaching job in 1995 with East Carolina. On May 15, 1995, Anne was inducted into the National Basketball Hall of Fame, and in 2004, she became the first female coach to capture a WNBA title. *Virginia Sports Hall of Fame 1996.*

SHARPSHOOTER DELL CURRY.
Born on June 25, 1964, Dell
Curry led the Fort Defiance
High cagers to the state
championship. At Virginia
Tech, Dell was a proficient
scorer who averaged 19 points
per game and was named All-
American and Metro
Conference Player of the Year in
1986. The pro ranks beckoned,
and the Harrisonburg native was
a first round pick of the Utah
Jazz and eventually suited up
with Cleveland, Charlotte,
Milwaukee, and Toronto over a
solid 16-year NBA career.
During his playing days, Dell was
the most feared three-point
shooter in the league and was
honored by the NBA with the
coveted Sixth Man of the Year
Award. *Virginia Sports Hall of
Fame 2004.*

CAGER BARRY PARKHILL. Born
and raised in Pennsylvania,
Barry Parkhill enrolled at the
University of Virginia in 1969
as a scholarship player and
quickly took the Atlantic Coast
Conference by storm. In his
junior year, Barry was named
ACC Athlete of the Year and
led the league in scoring.
Considered the commander for
the Cavaliers in the backcourt,
the two-time All-American led
UVA to a 21-7 record in 1972
and post-season play in the
NIT. Barry began a brief pro
career with the Virginia Squires
of the American Basketball
Association in 1973 and
remained with the league until
it folded at the end of the 1975-
1976 season. *Virginia Sports Hall
of Fame 2001.*

EARL "BIG CAT" LLOYD, PRO BASKETBALL'S JACKIE ROBINSON. Born in Alexandria on April 3, 1928, Earl Lloyd began his hardcourt career at Parker-Gray High where he earned numerous state and regional honors. After graduation, Earl initially followed his dream of pitching in the major leagues but refused to sign a contract from the Brooklyn Dodgers and entered college instead. At West Virginia State, he starred on the hardcourt and led his unbeaten team to the CIAA title in 1948. He eventually signed with the Washington Capitols, and on October 31, 1950, more than three years after Jackie Robinson broke the color line in baseball, Earl "Big Cat" Lloyd became the first African-American cager to play in the NBA. He later set records as the first African American to win an NBA Championship and also became the first of his race to be named assistant coach in the league. *Virginia Sports Hall of Fame 1993.*

CAGER COACH JULIUS CONN. From 1927 to 1953, Julius Conn led his Newport News High cagers to state titles in 1931, 1938, 1942–1943, and 1951–1952. While his accomplishments on the hardcourt are legendary, Julius also coached the school's track team and led them to numerous state championships under his guidance. In 1968, Julie Conn was named Coach of the Year by the National High School Coaches Association, an award well deserved for a lifetime of unparalleled commitment and accomplishment. After his retirement from prep coaching, the Newport News legend served in an administrative position with the Virginia Squires of the American Basketball Association. *Virginia Sports Hall of Fame 1976.*

DUAL-SPORT STAR GLEN KNOX. Considered by many to be one of the most gifted athletes in the history of William and Mary, Glen Charles Knox was a star on both the gridiron and the hardcourt for the Indians. A native of Niota, Tennessee, Glen transferred from Tennessee Wesleyan and enrolled at the Williamsburg college in 1940. As an end on the football squad, Glen led the Indians to the Southern Conference title in 1942 and was named to the All-Conference team. On the basketball court, the Tennessee native scored a record 359 points during the 1941–1942 season and was named to the All-Conference and All-State teams. The following season, he repeated these honors and was named Virginia State Player of the Year. *Virginia Sports Hall of Fame 1982.*

OLD DOMINION'S BASKETBALL DIVA, NANCY LIEBERMAN. As a teenager growing up in Far Rockaway, New York, Nancy Lieberman learned the art of basketball on the challenging asphalt courts of Harlem against some of the best ball handlers the city had to offer. Her early experiences surely paid off, as she became one of the most recognized and respected women to ever play the game. At Old Dominion University, Nancy led the Lady Monarchs to two consecutive AIAW national championships and one NWIT title. The scrappy cager and intelligent ball handler was a two-time winner of the Wade Trophy and a three-time All-American. Nancy played pro ball in both men's and women's leagues and was inducted into the National Basketball Hall of Fame in 1996. *Virginia Sports Hall of Fame 1992.*

NBA Veteran Allan Bristow. A native of Richmond, Allan Bristow first excelled on the hardcourt at Henrico High before enrolling at Virginia Tech. As a Hokie, Allan led Tech to its first National Invitational Tournament title and finished his collegiate career averaging 23 points per game. The 6-foot 7-inch forward was selected by the Philadelphia 76ers in the NBA draft and played two years in Philly before he was signed by the San Antonio Spurs of the American Basketball Association for the 1975–1976 season. His pro career spanned ten years until his retirement in 1983. Following his playing days, Allan was named as head coach of the Charlotte Hornets and later served as general manager for the New Orleans Hornets. *Virginia Sports Hall of Fame 1997.*

Charlie Mior. A native of North Carolina, Charlie Moir excelled in both basketball and baseball at Appalachian State University. Always a student of the game, Charlie began a memorable coaching career at the prep level and soon established his winning ways at several colleges, including Tulane, Roanoke, and Virginia Tech. While at Roanoke, his teams won 133 contests while losing only 44 during a 6-year period. In 1972, Roanoke captured the NCAA College Division Championship and Charlie was named National College Division Coach of the Year. *Virginia Sports Hall of Fame 2000.*

NORFOLK STATE'S BOBBY DANDRIDGE. Robert "Bobby" Dandridge was born in Richmond and began a memorable basketball career on the hardcourt of Maggie Walker High in 1962. At Norfolk State University, "Pick," as he was tagged by his Spartan teammates, was selected All-Central Intercollegiate Athletic Association (CIAA) from 1967 through 1969. Selected in the fourth round of the NBA draft by the Milwaukee Bucks, Bobby was named to the NBA All-Star squad four times and won championships with Milwaukee and Washington over his 12-year career. Following his days in the NBA, Bobby returned to the Tidewater area and served as assistant coach at Hampton University. The photo above shows Bobby in battle with Julius "Dr. J" Erving. *Virginia Sports Hall of Fame 1992.*

GLENN ROBERTS, FATHER OF THE MODERN-DAY JUMP SHOT. Born in Pound, Virginia, and known as the "Pound Pivoter," Glenn Roberts led his high school team to two state championships. Considered one of the pioneers of the game, Glenn is credited as being the first player to use the present-day jump shot. Over his four-year career at Emory and Henry, Glenn scored 1,531 points in 80 games and was named All-Conference and league MVP all four seasons. In 1935, Glenn was the first Virginia basketball player to be named to an All-American team. *Virginia Sports Hall of Fame 1980.*

HONORABLE JUNIUS KELLOGG. A talented athlete at I.C. Norcom High, Junius Kellogg excelled at basketball, track, football, and baseball. The Portsmouth native entered Manhattan College in 1949 as the school's first African-American player. While at school, he was offered a bribe to shave points. The honorable Junius informed his coach, and a national scandal was uncovered and revealed that 32 college players had fixed 86 games between 1947 and 1950. After graduation from Manhattan, Junius joined the Harlem Globetrotters, but an auto accident left him paralyzed. After years of rehab, Junius pioneered the sport of wheelchair basketball and coached the Pan Am Jets to a national title. *Virginia Sports Hall of Fame 1990.*

CAVALIER CENTER RALPH SAMPSON. As a University of Virginia Cavalier, Ralph Sampson was a four-time All-American and three-time National and Atlantic Coast Conference Player of the Year. With Ralph in control of the paint, UVA captured the NIT championship in his freshman year and made three NCAA post-season appearances. With his college career over, the Harrisonburg native was selected as the No. 1 pick in the NBA by the Houston Rockets and quickly put together an impressive inaugural season with a 21-point average. Ralph's NBA career spanned nine seasons and included stints with four teams before knee injuries forced his retirement. In the above photograph, Ralph puts the move on Tarheel cagers Michael Jordan and Sam Perkins. *Virginia Sports Hall of Fame 1996.*

COACH PAUL WEBB MOTIVATES THE MONARCHS. A graduate of William and Mary, Paul Webb (in dark jacket, right) amassed 511 victories as a college head coach for two Virginia schools. From 1956 to 1975, Paul guided Randolph-Macon to 315 victories and captured the first Mason-Dixon championship trophy by a Virginia school. At Old Dominion, Paul guided the 1976–1977 Monarchs to a 22-game winning streak and set a number of records in the process. Pictured alongside Coach Webb is his son, ODU assistant coach Eddie Webb, the executive director of the Virginia Sports Hall of Fame. *Virginia Sports Hall of Fame 1993.*

ROBERT "BOB" KILBOURNE. Born and raised in Big Stone Gap, Virginia, Bob Kilbourne entered Emory and Henry College on a football scholarship in 1940 but soon established himself as one of the school's all-time great basketball players. The Virginia native was picked All-State and led the commonwealth in scoring over his junior and senior years. Following his days on the hardcourt, Bob coached throughout the state and brought a unique brand of leadership to each institution with which he was associated over his career. *Virginia Sports Hall of Fame 1997.*

SUPER SQUIRE DAVE TWARDZIK. A two-time All-American at Old Dominion, Dave Twardzik was the Monarch's leader and playmaker during his three-year varsity career at the Norfolk school. In 1972, Dave began a pro career with the ABA Virginia Squires and was selected as an All-Star in 1975. After the collapse of the ABA in 1976, Dave was picked up by Portland and proved to be one of the surest shots in the NBA as he knocked in 61.2 percent of field goal attempts and led the Trailblazers to the 1976–1977 league championship. Once retired, Dave remained active in the game and served as a scout, radio analyst and front office administrator for a number of NBA teams. *Virginia Sports Hall of Fame 1995*.

Norfolk Native and NCAA Coaching Legend Lefty Driesell. In early January 2003, Charles "Lefty" Driesell announced his retirement as a basketball coach after 49 seasons of guiding young men at the high school and college level. The "Old Left-Hander," as he was known by many, took his first coaching position at Norfolk's Granby High and later led Newport News High to an undefeated 25-0 season and state championship. At Duke University, Lefty excelled on the hardcourt as a player and later returned to his home state to earn a master's degree at William and Mary. His collegiate coaching career began with Davidson in 1960 and ended with Georgia State on a cold January morning in 2003. During his many seasons of college coaching, Lefty amassed 786 wins with Davidson, Maryland, James Madison, and Georgia State. *Virginia Sports Hall of Fame 1995.*

VIRGINIA SPORTS HALL OF FAME NOTABLES
Additional "Heroes of the Hardcourt" Inductees

◆ **J. DALLAS SHIRLEY.** The first ever Virginia Sports Hall of Fame inductee to be honored for a career as an athletic official, Dallas presided over more than 2,000 basketball games for 30-plus years. *Virginia Sports Hall of Fame 1985.*

◆ **LESTER HOOKER.** Born in Stuart, Les Hooker became a star cager at Richmond's Thomas Jefferson High and later excelled on the hardcourt and diamond for William and Mary. Following his playing days, Les led the Tribe to 156 wins as a head coach and later served as the school's athletic director. *Virginia Sports Hall of Fame 1983.*

◆ **JIMMIE BRYAN.** A legendary coach and athletic director at E.G. Glass High in Lynchburg for more than 50 years, Jimmie led his prep cagers to four Virginia AAA Championships and 22 District Championships. *Virginia Sports Hall of Fame 1987.*

◆ **HERMAN "BUCKY" KELLER.** A native of Newport News, Bucky Keller was a multi-talented sports star for Newport News High and led the Typhoons to the Virginia State basketball championship for three consecutive years from 1956 to 1958. He continued his excellence on the hardcourt at Virginia Tech and averaged 18.2 points per game and grabbed more than 7 rebounds per contest. *Virginia Sports Hall of Fame 1992.*

◆ **CHARLES H. WILLIAMS.** A graduate of Hampton Institute in 1909, Charles Holston Williams was one of the original founders of the Central Intercollegiate Athletic Association (CIAA). Charles was a longtime athletic director at Hampton, a position he held from 1909 until his retirement in 1951. *Virginia Sports Hall of Fame 1981.*

◆ **ALBERT "RASTY" DORAN.** A legendary basketball coach at Alexandria's George Washington High, Rasty accumulated 534 victories over a remarkable career. From 1938 through 1953, he led his prep cagers to more than 15 Northern Virginia titles and the 1944–1945 Virginia State Group I crown. *Virginia Sports Hall of Fame 1995.*

◆ **BILL CHAMBERS.** A native of Lynchburg, Bill Chambers led the E.G. Glass cagers to an undefeated season and a state championship. As a collegiate, Bill was a dominant force for William and Mary and was named All-State, All-Southern Conference, and All-American. Following his playing days, he coached the Newport News High basketball team to state championships in 1956 and again in 1957. Bill returned to William and Mary and served as a respected and successful coach for the Tribe for nine seasons. *Virginia Sports Hall of Fame 1995.*

VIRGINIA'S MOST GIFTED ATHLETE, ARTHUR ASHE. Whether it was his stand against apartheid in South Africa in the 1970s, his fight to eradicate illiteracy, or his AIDS public awareness campaign, Arthur Robert Ashe Jr. made a profound and remarkable impact on the people of the world. Born in 1943, Arthur was first taught the game of tennis on Richmond's Brookfield Park courts under the guidance of Dr. Walter Johnson and by 1963 became the first African American to join the U.S. Davis Cup team. As a student at UCLA, Arthur led the Bruin tennis squad to the NCAA team title and captured the men's national singles championship. Arthur reached the No. 1 position in pro tennis in 1968 and again in 1975, when he won the men's singles title at Wimbledon. *Virginia Sports Hall of Fame 1979.*

FIVE

A Collage of Champions

This chapter showcases the wide range of exceptional athletes who made names for themselves outside the big three categories of sports of baseball, football, and basketball. Consider the wide array of sports that are represented in this chapter: golf, wrestling, equestrian riding, boxing, bowling, swimming, automobile racing, track and field, speedboat racing, gymnastics, yachting, field hockey, tennis, soccer, rowing, thoroughbred racing, and surfing. We also should not forget the coaches and administrators who taught, mentored, and guided the many fine athletes in their quest for perfection in these sports.

Many larger-than-life legends familiar to the average sports fan hailed from Virginia or perfected their craft in the commonwealth. Of all the inductees in the Virginia Sports Hall of Fame, no one earned more respect on and off the court than Richmond native Arthur Ashe. His dominance in tennis was only eclipsed by his humanitarian efforts to bring equality and social change to every person with whom he came into contact throughout his life. When the legends of the links are mentioned, Sam Snead is on everyone's most admired list, for the native Virginian still holds many PGA records and will be remembered as golf's most approachable and likeable hacker. Beside Snead, many other Virginians were golfers of merit and include such legends as Chandler Harper, Lew Worsham, Vinny Giles, Lanny Watkins, Wynsol Spencer, Curtis Strange, J.C. Snead, Donna Andrews, Mary Patton Janssen, Lilly Harper Martin, Tom Strange, Robbye King Unger, and Richard Alphonso Smith.

There are more than a few great Virginia athletes who became legends in their own time. When the early days of NASCAR are discussed, such names as Curtis "Pops" Turner, "Lil' Joe" Weatherly, and Wendell Scott are spoken with reverence, just as much for their accomplishments on the track as for their personalities and strength of character. The frenzy of NASCAR in much of the state can be linked to Hall of Famer Paul Sawyer and his dedication in the establishment and expansion of the Richmond International Speedway.

The international stage of the Olympics has showcased more than a few talented Virginians, including wrestler Gray Simons; swimmers Thompson Mann, Melissa Belote-Ripley, and Shelly Mann; track star Benita Fitzgerald-Mosley; gymnast Hope Spivey; field hockey legend Yogi Hightower-Boothe; and canoer Frank Havens, to name only a few.

There are numerous stories of interest to be discovered within the profiles of the many legends portrayed within this chapter. One such tale surrounds the legacy of Portsmouth native Dick Shea, who excelled at track and field at West Point. Shea was awarded the nation's highest honor, the Congressional Medal of Honor, for his leadership and heroics at Pork Chop Hill during the Korean War, when he made the ultimate sacrifice as a young army lieutenant.

Besides the accomplished athletes included in this chapter, the careers of their mentors are also noted. Some of these special individuals include Dr. Robert "Whirlwind" Johnson, the guiding force behind such great African-American tennis legends as Althea Gibson and Arthur Ashe, track and field coach Archie Hahn, and soccer coach Bill Shellenberger, to name only a few. The coaches honored in this chapter provided their athletes with the guidance to make them champions on and off the competitive field.

While the more recognized names of the world of sports will be familiar to the reader, take the time to explore the lesser-known individuals within this chapter. They are the ones who made Virginia what it is today, a collage of champions.

VINNY GILES, GOLF'S TOP AMATEUR. A native of Lynchburg, Vinny Giles loved golf, vowing to "never play for pay," and kept his amateur status throughout his career on the links. Vinny won his first Virginia amateur trophy in 1962, and by his final win in 1971, he held the coveted cup aloft a total of six times. In 1972, the Virginian captured the U.S. Amateur and won the British Amateur in 1975. *Virginia Sports Hall of Fame 1976.*

WRESTLING CHAMP GRAY SIMONS. Born in Norfolk, Gray Simons was a student of legendary wrestling coach Billy Martin Sr. at Granby High School. After he captured the prep state championship at Granby, Gray attended Lock Haven State and amassed an amazing record of 91-2. He was crowned NCAA champion three times and NAIA champ four times for a total of seven titles, a feat that has never been matched. The Norfolk native was a two-time Olympian and placed just out of reach for a medal in 1960 and 1964. Gray held coaching positions at the U.S. Military Academy, Lock Haven, Indiana State, Tennessee, and Old Dominion University. Gray was inducted into the National Wrestling Hall of Fame in 1978. *Virginia Sports Hall of Fame 1992.*

SLAMMIN' SAM SNEAD, VIRGINIA'S DOWN HOME GOLF LEGEND. Given the nickname "Slammin' Sam" for his lengthy fairway drives, Samuel Jackson Snead was born in the mountains of Virginia in 1912 and began caddying at a young age. Once accepted into the pro circuit, Sam put together a remarkable career as he amassed a PGA record of 81 tour victories with just as many worldwide wins on his resume. In regard to major wins, he was awarded trophies for the Masters and the PGA Championship three times each and the British Open once. Sam Snead will be remembered for his folksy manner, his relaxed approach to the game, and his trademark straw hat. *Virginia Sports Hall of Fame 1973.*

PGA Champ Lanny Wadkins.
Born in Richmond, Lanny Wadkins honed his skills on the links for Meadowbrook High and later Wake Forest University. In the early 1970s, Lanny captured the U.S. Amateur title and won the Southern Amateur championship twice. Once on the pro circuit, Lanny won 21 PGA tournaments over 27 years on the tour. In 1977, he captured the PGA Championship in a playoff with Gene Littler and added the 1979 Tournament of Players title to his ever-impressive resume. In 1985, the Virginian was awarded golf's highest honor when he was named PGA Player of the Year. *Virginia Sports Hall of Fame 1996.*

Jean McLean-Davis, Queen of the Saddle.
Jean McLean-Davis seized her first major championship at Madison Square Garden at the tender age of 12. By the time she reached 14, Jean won her first World Grand Championship and recaptured the cup at the age of 16 and 17. Specializing in the Three-Gaited and Five-Gaited Stakes, this legend has won over 65 World Grand Championships while her stable in Kentucky has added another 845 to her trophy case. *Virginia Sports Hall of Fame 1976.*

VIRGINIA'S MOST VERSATILE ATHLETE, HERBERT BRYANT. Born in Alexandria, Herb Bryant, lettered in four sports at Episcopal High. At the University of Virginia, he excelled in a variety of sports, including football, basketball, baseball, track, and boxing and was the first freshman at the school to letter in four sports. In 1931 and 1932, Herb was All-American and All-Southern in football, and on the track, he captured the state title in the shot put and discus throw. Pictured above in a classic pose, Herb proved to be a tough heavyweight pugilist and captured the Southern Conference title in his first season as a collegiate. *Virginia Sports Hall of Fame 1984.*

DUCKPIN CHAMP DORIS LEIGH. The golden era of duckpin bowling was ruled by Virginian Doris Leigh. From the late 1940s through the decade of the 1950s, there was no one better at the sport than she. A champion of numerous tournaments, this queen of the alley won the National Singles title in 1949 and the National All-Events in 1950. Doris was ranked the No. 1 duckpin bowler in the United States in 1957 and again in 1958. *Virginia Sports Hall of Fame 1978.*

OLYMPIAN THOMPSON MANN. Born in Hickory and raised in Chesapeake, Thompson Mann developed into a world-class swimmer at Great Bridge High. After graduation, he entered the University of North Carolina and earned All-American status twice over a remarkable collegiate career. Thompson was the first to swim the 100-meter backstroke in under a minute as recorded in the opening leg of the USA's gold medal–winning medley relay at the 1964 Olympics. Over his career, Thompson held two world records, four American records, and several AAU backstroke titles. *Virginia Sports Hall of Fame 1988.*

NORFOLK'S NASCAR KING, 'LIL JOE WEATHERLY. Born on May 29, 1922, in Norfolk, Joe Weatherly first showed a love for motor sports when he was hired to deliver goods for a local pharmacy on a second-hand scooter. By 15, he acquired his first motorcycle and began to race and win on the local dirt tracks. Following a tour in the military, in which he suffered a facial wound, Joe began to race professionally on the American Motorcycle Association circuit and won several national titles in the late 1940s. The following season, 'Lil Joe began to race late-model cars on the pro circuit and was named NASCAR champion in 1962 and 1963. On January 19, 1964, at the age of 41, Joe Weatherly was killed in a crash during a race in California at the height of his popularity. *Virginia Sports Hall of Fame 1976.*

GOLFER WYNSOL SPENCER.
Raised in Newport News, Wynsol
Spencer captured five Virginia
Amateur championships over a
span of two decades. During a
stellar amateur golfing career,
Wynsol scored 28 holes-in-one on
the links. *Virginia Sports Hall of
Fame 1991.*

PGA CHAMP LEW WORSHAM.
Over a respectable PGA career,
Lew Worsham captured six titles
on the pro tour, three Mid-
Atlantic trophies, and two Tri-
State tournaments. The crafty
Virginian first showed interest in
golf at Hampton High before
serving as head professional at
various clubs on the East Coast.
Virginia Sports Hall of Fame 1986.

BENITA FITZGERALD-MOSLEY, DALE CITY'S OLYMPIC SPEEDSTER. Benita Fitzgerald first set the track and field world on fire in 1979 when she broke the USA National High School record in the 100-yard dash with a time of 10.6 seconds. From there, the Virginian attended the University of Tennessee and specialized in the hurdles and short dashes. Benita's speed qualified her for a spot on the 1980 and 1984 U.S. Olympic teams. During the 1984 Olympic Games, Benita won the gold medal in the 100-meter hurdles and became the first African-American woman to win the top prize in this event. *Virginia Sports Hall of Fame 1998.*

LEGEND HENRY LAUTERBACH. Born in Norfolk and raised in Newport News, Henry Lauterbach is known for his speed on the water and state-of-the-art boat designs. During the 1950s, Henry dominated the sport of speedboat racing and won national titles in 1954 and 1956. His boat, the *Miss Washington*, with its 266-cubic-inch engine, gave him such an advantage that he captured 51 of 52 races. In 1959, Henry returned with his famous boat the *Wa Wa* and won a national championship for the third time in his illustrious career. *Virginia Sports Hall of Fame 1999.*

"STUKIE" HOSKINS. At Fredericksburg High, Stuart "Stukie" Hoskins was awarded 14 letters for excellence in football, basketball, baseball, and track. Stukie entered the University of Richmond in 1936 and earned All-State status in football and baseball for the Spiders. *Virginia Sports Hall of Fame 1981.*

ONE OF AMERICA'S GREATEST SWIMMERS, MELISSA BELOTE-RIPLEY. Born on October 16, 1956, in the nation's capital and raised in Springfield, Virginia, Melissa Belote is considered one of America's greatest competitive swimmers. At the young age of 12, she qualified for her first United States Championship, and by the age of 15, she earned a spot on the U.S. Olympic squad. At the 1972 games in Munich, Melissa won gold medals in the 100-meter backstroke, the 200-meter backstroke, and the team relay. At Arizona State, she captured six National Collegiate Swimming titles and was named All-American four times. *Virginia Sports Hall of Fame 1989.*

OLYMPIC GYMNAST HOPE SPIVEY.
Raised in Suffolk, Hope Spivey moved
to Allentown, Pennsylvania, at the
age of 13 to prepare herself for a career
in gymnastics. In 1987, Hope was a
member of America's gold medal
winning team at the Pan Am games
and placed fourth at the 1988
Olympics, just missing the bronze by
the slimmest of margins. At the
University of Georgia, she reigned as
the NCAA's all-time national record
holder for the most perfect 10s in her
routines and reached the often
untouchable pinnacle an amazing 27
times. In 1991, Hope Spivey was
named the "Top Female Collegiate
Gymnast" in the country. *Virginia
Sports Hall of Fame 2004.*

SAILING LEGEND "DINK" VAIL. At
the young age of 10, Charles "Dink"
Vail began a remarkable career on the
water when he first crewed for his
older brother on the family's small
sailboat. By the age of 12, Dink won
his first trophy as he bested the fleet
in a local Hampton Roads regatta.
The Norfolk native graduated from
Maury High and attended Virginia
Tech before he enlisted in the Coast
Guard during the Korean War. From
1943 to 1967, he won more than 100
regattas and captured the national
championship in 1964 in the Flying
Dutchman and Jollyboat classes. Dink
was the founding father of the world-
renowned sailing team at Old
Dominion University. *Virginia Sports
Hall of Fame 1985.*

THREE-TIME PGA PLAYER OF THE YEAR CURTIS STRANGE. At the young age of 15, Curtis Strange had already made his mark in golf when he captured the Virginia Junior Championship. As a collegiate at Wake Forest, he was a three-time All-American and led the Demon Deacons to the NCAA championship trophy in 1974 and again in 1975. During the 1980s, Curtis was named the PGA's top money winner three times and was the first golfer to win more than $1 million on the tour. In an amazing feat that had not been duplicated since the days of Ben Hogan, Curtis won back-to-back U.S. Open titles in 1988 and 1989. To top off his incredible career on the links, the hard-driving Virginian was named PGA Player of the Year in 1985, 1987, and 1988. *Virginia Sports Hall of Fame 2004.*

ROANOKE CAGER PAUL RICE. A multi-talented athlete at Roanoke College, Paul Rice excelled on the hardcourt as well as the tennis court. During the 1930s, Paul was part of the famous "Five Smart Boys" (page 4) that led Roanoke to back-to-back state basketball championships. At the National Intercollegiate Tournament, he was named top scorer and elected to the All-Tournament team. Paul was also the school's star tennis player and excelled on the diamond, where he played centerfield and batted cleanup. *Virginia Sports Hall of Fame 1988.*

JOHN MAPP. Born in Portsmouth and raised in Norfolk, John Mapp was a multi-sport star at Granby High and continued his legacy on the athletic fields at Virginia Military Institute. On the gridiron, John was named All-State, All-Southern, and All-American. He was also honored as Football Player of the Year in Virginia during his senior year. On the track, John would often outscore the opposing teams by himself and won five events per meet on a regular basis. *Virginia Sports Hall of Fame 1991.*

CURTIS "POPS" TURNER, A LEGEND IN HIS OWN TIME. Born in Floyd, Virginia, on April 12, 1924, Curtis Turner was an experienced lumberman by day and a storied moonshine runner on dark country roads at night. While the nighttime antics were never substantiated, the story lends itself to the legend of Curtis Turner as motor racing's most charismatic driver of all time. Curtis began his pro racing career after his discharge from the military and won his first NASCAR Winston Cup race, known as the Grand National, in 1949. He earned his nickname of "Pops" for his talent to knock and pop drivers off the course with regularity. Over his career as a driver, promoter, and racetrack builder, he won more than 380 races and posted 17 Winston Cup victories. Curtis Morton "Pops" Turner's life ended on October 4, 1970, when a plane in which he was a passenger crashed in Punxsutawney, Pennsylvania. *Virginia Sports Hall of Fame 1999.*

YOGI HIGHTOWER-BOOTHE. A gifted athlete at Kempsville High and later Old Dominion, Yogi Hightower developed into one of the most dynamic field hockey players in the nation. Her talents with the stick earned her back-to-back All-American honors with the Lady Monarchs. Yogi was named a 1984 Olympic alternate and earned a starting position on the field hockey squad for the 1988 games. *Virginia Sports Hall of Fame 2001.*

TENNIS CHAMPION HAL BURROWS. Hal Burrows started collecting trophies at a young age when he captured the Virginia State Boys Championship from 1938 to 1939 and took the junior title from 1941 to 1942. As a student at the University of Virginia, he won three Virginia State Championships. *Virginia Sports Hall of Fame 1990.*

BILL SHELLENBERGER. Over a span of 45 years, Soccer Hall of Fame member Bill Shellenberger led his Lynchburg College kickers to 371 victories and 31 consecutive winning seasons. This amazing coach won numerous state championships and produced 11 All-Americans over his career. *Virginia Sports Hall of Fame 1998.*

SHELLY MANN, OVERCOMING THE ODDS. Born on Long Island and stricken with polio at an early age, Shelly Mann received treatment involving aqua therapy and learning how to swim. By the age of 12, she started to swim competitively, and as a student at Washington-Lee High in Arlington, this amazing teenager set world records in the pool. In the early 1950s, Shelly won the U.S. Championship in more than six classes, and at the 1956 Olympics, she was awarded a gold medal in the butterfly and a silver in the 400-meter freestyle medley. *Virginia Sports Hall of Fame 1984.*

MENTOR ROBERT JOHNSON. Born in Norfolk, Robert Johnson earned All-American status in 1924 as a member of Lincoln University's football squad and was nicknamed "Whirlwind" for his prowess on the gridiron. He also excelled at tennis and during his career won more than 50 trophies and 6 national championships. Dr. Johnson exposed thousands of disadvantaged children to the game of tennis and was the personal mentor for such legends as Althea Gibson and Arthur Ashe. *Virginia Sports Hall of Fame 1972.*

CHAMPION PEGGY AUGUSTUS. Born in Cleveland and a longtime resident of Keswick, Virginia, Peggy Augustus was one of the most successful riders of show horses from 1950 through 1965. During this era, Peggy won every major title throughout the United States and Canada, including the National Horse Show at Madison Square Garden, the Devon Horse Show, and the Royal Winter Fair. Following her riding career, she developed one of the most respected breeding and racing programs in the country for Thoroughbreds at her Keswick stables. *Virginia Sports Hall of Fame 1999.*

THE "MILWAUKEE METEOR," ARCHIE HAHN. Born on September 14, 1880, in Dodgeville, Wisconsin, Archibald "Archie" Hahn was one of the best world-class sprinters at the turn of the century. As an undergraduate at the University of Michigan, the young track and field star made Olympic history when he won the 60-, 100-, and 200-meter sprints at the St. Louis games of 1904. He also ran a world record time in the 200-meter run and captured the AAU National Championship in the 100-yard and 220-yard events. Nicknamed the "Milwaukee Meteor," Archie received a law degree from Michigan but never practiced; instead, he found a career in coaching more to his liking. In 22 years at the University of Virginia, Archie guided the Cavaliers to 12 track and field state championships and 56 dual meet victories. *Virginia Sports Hall of Fame 1991.*

PGA Champ J.C. Snead. J.C. Snead had all goods to be an elite baseball player and eventually worked his way through the Washington Senators minor league system with his hopes set on a major league career. Once he decided to put down the bat and pick up an iron, the sweet swinging Virginian never looked back. In 1964, J.C., the nephew of golf legend Sam Snead, began to emulate his famous relative and within three years earned a card on the PGA tour. Over the next 22 years, the Bath County native won 8 regular PGA tournaments and another 4 on the Senior Tour. *Virginia Sports Hall of Fame 2003.*

Gold Medalist Frank Havens. A native of Arlington and longtime resident of Virginia's eastern shore, Frank Havens was a multi-talented athlete at Washington and Lee High. While his exploits on the gridiron earned him rave reviews, Frank gave up the game to become a four-time Olympian in the sport of canoeing. During the 1952 games in Helsinki, Frank won the grueling 10,000-meter single-blade race and was awarded the gold medal after setting a new world record. Interestingly, Frank's father passed over the chance to compete in the 1924 Olympics and chose to remain at home to await the birth of his future gold medal–winning son. In an appropriate show of respect and gratitude, Frank Havens presented the gold medal to his father when he returned home. *Virginia Sports Hall of Fame 1995.*

GRANBY HIGH SCHOOL WRESTLING LEGEND BILLY MARTIN SR. Born in Beaufort, North Carolina, Billy Martin began an illustrious wrestling career on the mats of Michigan State under the direction of legend Walter Jacobs. His coaching career originated at Norfolk's Granby High, and during his tenure, the Comets captured an amazing 22 state championships and produced 106 individual state wrestling champions. An innovator in the sport, Billy was the originator of the world-famous "Granby Series" of wrestling moves that is still held in high esteem today. William Patrick "Billy" Martin Sr. was named a Distinguished Member of the National Wrestling Hall of Fame in 1980. *Virginia Sports Hall of Fame 1980.*

SPIDER START CHUCK BOONE. An All-State football player at Covington High, Chuck Boone proved to be a champion in all sports and continued his athletic prowess at the University of Richmond. After graduation, he chose a career in baseball over one on the gridiron and signed with the New York Yankees. Once he hung up his glove and left the professional ranks, Chuck returned to his alma mater and served with distinction as baseball coach and director of athletics for more than 20 years. *Virginia Sports Hall of Fame 2004.*

TENNIS CHAMPION DONNA FLOYD FALES. A native of Atlanta, Donna Floyd and her family moved to Arlington in 1953. As a teenager, she was recognized as the top-ranked player in the country for her age and won the U.S. Girls 15 and Under National Championship. Donna graduated from William and Mary in 1962 and flirted with a No. 1 international ranking during the 1960s with quarterfinal finishes at the French Open, the United States Open, and Wimbledon. She served on the Wightman Cup team in 1963 and 1964 and is a member of the Women's Collegiate Tennis Hall of Fame. *Virginia Sports Hall of Fame 1997.*

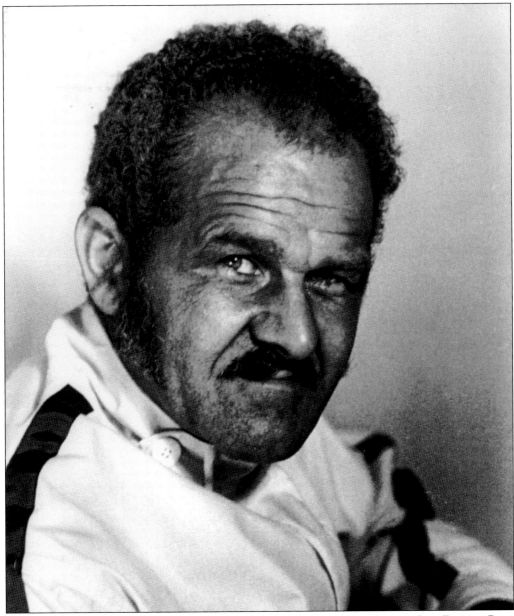

WENDELL SCOTT, THE NATION'S FIRST AFRICAN-AMERICAN PRO STOCK CAR RACER. Born in Danville, Wendell Scott became the first man of his race to formally compete on the pro stock car circuit when he entered to run on Richmond's old quarter-mile track in 1952. Despite obvious attempts by drivers to bump him off the track, Wendell prevailed and won the race. He entered the Grand National circuit in 1961 and earned his first trophy two years later as he finished four laps ahead of his nearest challenger. Despite the clear win, Wendell was not declared the victor and demanded a recount. After a recalculation of the judges' scorecards, he was named the winner. During an illustrious racing career that eventually earned him the respect of the other drivers on the circuit, Wendell achieved 128 wins in 506 Grand National starts. His career on the racetrack and his battle against prejudice was made into a 1977 film titled *Greased Lightning. Virginia Sports Hall of Fame 2000.*

VIRGINIA BEACH SURFING LEGEND BOB HOLLAND. The son of a harbor pilot and early surfing pioneer on the East Coast, Virginia Beach native Bob Holland Jr. began his foray into riding the waves at an early age. In 1955, the young entrepreneur sold surfboards out of the family's garage and opened Virginia Beach's first surf shop seven years later with friend Pete Smith. Over a career filled with trophies and accomplishments, Bob has captured the U.S. Surfing Championship seven times and is the only winner to achieve this feat on all three continental coasts. In 1963, he was the founding father of the East Coast Surfing Championships, which is staged annually in Virginia Beach, and took the trophy himself 10 times. *Virginia Sports Hall of Fame 1997.*

IDA SIMMONS SLACK. With her first attempt at bowling in the early 1930s, Ida Simmons Slack soon found that she possessed a special talent for the sport. By 1934, the Norfolk native was ranked No. 1 in the nation for duckpin bowling and remained atop the rankings consistently through 1940. She was the first duckpin bowler in the nation to turn pro and remained active in the sport through the 1950s. Fittingly, Ida Simmons Slack was included in the inaugural group of bowlers to be inducted in the Duckpin National Hall of Fame in 1961. *Virginia Sports Hall of Fame 1982.*

TRIBE TRACK START "MONK" LITTLE AND COACH "SCRAP" CHANDLER. A native of Norfolk, Henry "Monk" Little (left) excelled at the long jump, javelin throw, and 100-, 220-, and 440-yard dash at William and Mary. Monk set five collegiate Virginia State Records over his career and still holds the William and Mary record of 25 feet in the long jump. Shown alongside Monk is his longtime coach and mentor Joseph C. "Scrap" Chandler (right). An outstanding William and Mary athlete in his own right, Scrap later coached 44 years at the collegiate level. Upon leaving Williamsburg, Scrap became a respected athletic director and coach at Old Dominion, staying until 1968. Monk Little was inducted into the Virginia Sports Hall of Fame in 1975, while Scrap Chandler joined him four years later.

HYDRO-PLANE CHAMP BOB ROWLAND. A native of Chesapeake, Bob Rowland excelled in golf and track at William and Mary. After graduation, he began to explore the new sport of speedboat racing and by 1951 was named "Outstanding Speed Boat Racing Driver in America." During a remarkable career on the water, Bob won the 1951–1952 President's Cup Regatta in Washington and the National Sweepstakes in 1952 and is a member of the National Marine Racing Hall of Fame. *Virginia Sports Hall of Fame 1978.*

ARMY HERO DICK SHEA. Born in Portsmouth, Dick Shea was a gifted athlete at Churchland High before he entered Virginia Tech. After service as an enlisted man in World War II, Dick was accepted into West Point and began to run long distance. During his time as a cadet, he won the national cross-country championship and was considered one of the top mile runners in the country. As graduation approached, Dick was invited to become a member of the Olympic team but instead entered the army as a second lieutenant. With the Korean Conflict underway, Dick was given a platoon and found himself engaged in the legendary battle of Pork Chop Hill. On July 8, 1953, Dick Shea was killed as he led his troops into battle and was posthumously awarded the Medal of Honor. *Virginia Sports Hall of Fame 1987.*

GOLF LEGEND CHANDLER HARPER. A graduate of Portsmouth's Wilson High, Chandler Harper excelled on the diamond as well as the links for the Presidents. After graduation, he captured the Virginia Amateur in 1930, 1932, and 1933 with relative ease. Chandler turned pro after World War II and won 7 PGA championships and finished second in 13 others over a remarkable career. His résumé also includes a record 10 victories at the Virginia State Open and several wins on the PGA senior tour. In 1969, Chandler Harper was inducted into the PGA Hall of Fame. *Virginia Sports Hall of Fame 1973.*

LPGA Champ Donna Andrews. Born in Lynchburg, Donna Andrews developed into a successful golfer as a two-time Virginia State Junior Champion and a five-time Virginia Women's State Amateur champ in the 1980s. She joined the Ladies Professional Golf Association in 1989 and was named the 1990 Rookie of the Year. Donna captured her first major at the 1994 Nabisco Dinah Shore Classic and has six LPGA victories to her credit. The sweet-swinging Virginian has served as president of the LPGA and has been a longtime member of its executive committee. *Virginia Sports Hall of Fame 2005.*

Coach Ted Keller. For more than 50 years, Ted Keller has been a leader in athletics throughout the state of Virginia. As a student-athlete at Randolph-Macon College, Ted was a four-year starter and captured All-Mason-Dixon honors in 1952 and 1953 in football and baseball. As a coach at Randolph-Macon, Ted produced a 105-56-5 record and led the Yellow Jackets to seven football championships in the Mason-Dixon and ODAC. His 1969 squad won the Knute Rockne Bowl and was named national small college champions of the East. Ted was voted Virginia's small college Coach of the Year four times and ODAC Coach of the Year on three occasions. *Virginia Sports Hall of Fame 2005.*

Virginia Sports Hall of Fame Notables
Additional "Champions of the Commonwealth" Inductees

- **Gracie Lee VanDyck.** A multi-talented athlete at James Madison, Gracie VanDyck was a pioneer in women's sports and one of Virginia's most respected coaches for more than four decades at the high school level. *Virginia Sports Hall of Fame 2002.*

- **Melvin Blassingham.** Known as the "Father of the Oyster Bowl," Melvin Blassingham conceived the idea for a special bowl game to be played in Norfolk when he was hospitalized following a heart attack in 1936. *Virginia Sports Hall of Fame 1982.*

- **Terry Holland.** A legendary basketball coach at the University of Virginia for 16 seasons, Terry Holland compiled an impressive record of 326-173 and led the Cavaliers to NCAA post-season play eight times and the Final Four twice. *Virginia Sports Hall of Fame 2003.*

- **Laura Mapp.** In 37 years at Bridgewater College, Laura Mapp accumulated 876 victories as head coach of the women's basketball, field hockey, and tennis squads. *Virginia Sports Hall of Fame 2003.*

- **C.P. "Sally" Miles.** This early Virginia Tech gridiron coach was instrumental in the creation of many athletic programs at the Blacksburg school and served as first president of the Southern Conference. *Virginia Sports Hall of Fame 1974.*

- **Leotus "Lee" Morrison.** A successful women's coach and athletic director at James Madison University, Lee Morrison was a founding member of the Association for Intercollegiate Athletics for Women (AIAW) and served on the executive board of the United States Olympic Committee. *Virginia Sports Hall of Fame 2000.*

- **Frank O. Moseley.** A native of Alabama, Frank Moseley was named collegiate Coach of the Year in 1954 as he led his Virginia Tech football team to an undefeated 8-0-1 season. *Virginia Sports Hall of Fame 1979.*

- **Dick Price.** A legend as coach and athletic director at Norfolk State University for more than 40 years, Dick Price has garnered numerous awards in recognition of his leadership on and off the field. *Virginia Sports Hall of Fame 2001.*

- **Russell Potts.** The hall's first inductee to be enshrined for his contributions as a sports marketing specialist, Russ Potts staged more than 650 events over his career. Russ served as vice president of the Chicago White Sox and was elected to the Senate of Virginia in 1992. *Virginia Sports Hall of Fame 2004.*

- **Warren Rutledge.** A former pitcher with the Richmond Virginians, Warren Rutledge was a legendary basketball coach at Benedictine High School for 43 years with 949 victories to his credit. *Virginia Sports Hall of Fame 2001.*

- **Dr. Caroline B. Sinclair.** Sinclair was a pioneer at James Madison University in her support of women's athletics. *Virginia Sports Hall of Fame 1996.*

- **Bob Thalman.** A respected gridiron coach, Thalman served Virginia Military Institute and Hampden-Sydney College for 47 years. *Virginia Sports Hall of Fame 2003.*

VIRGINIA SPORTS HALL OF FAME NOTABLES
Additional "Champions of the Commonwealth" Inductees

- **E.P. "CY" TWOMBLY.** One of the founding fathers of intercollegiate athletics at Washington and Lee University, Cy Twombly coached the Generals to more than 400 victories in swimming and golf. *Virginia Sports Hall of Fame 1991.*

- **PAUL SAWYER.** A pioneer of modern day NASCAR, Paul Sawyer and driver Joe Weatherly leased a small dirt track in 1983 that eventually transformed into the 103,000-seat Richmond International Raceway. *Virginia Sports Hall of Fame 2002.*

- **MARY PATTON JANSSEN.** From 1957 through 1962, this Charlottesville resident was the state's most proficient female golfer as she captured state amateur women's titles six consecutive years. *Virginia Sports Hall of Fame 2001.*

- **LILLY HARPER MARTIN.** Sister of golfing legend Chandler Harper, Lilly was a dominant force in amateur golf as she posted victories at the Virginia State Women's Golf Championship seven times. *Virginia Sports Hall of Fame 1995.*

- **TOM STRANGE.** A student of the great Sam Snead, Tom appeared in six U. S. Opens and won five Virginia State Open titles in his career. *Virginia Sports Hall of Fame 1998.*

- **ROBBYE KING UNGER.** A dominant figure in golf throughout the state during the 1960s and 1970s, Robbye won six Virginia Women's Amateur Championships, three District of Columbia titles, and three Mid-Atlantic cups. *Virginia Sports Hall of Fame 1997.*

- **CHRISTOPHER CHENERY.** One of the most prominent figures in the world of horse racing, Christopher developed a 2,000-acre farm in Hanover County into the internationally renowned The Meadow. His facility produced a number of Thoroughbred legends, including Secretariat. *Virginia Sports Hall of Fame 1985.*

- **PAUL MELLON.** Owner and developer of the world-famous Rokeby Stables in Upperville, Virginia, Paul produced over 1,000 winners of stakes races. His stable produced 1993 Kentucky Derby winner Sea Hero. *Virginia Sports Hall of Fame 1999.*

- **JAMES DRIVER.** An excellent athlete who excelled in football, baseball, basketball, and track at William and Mary and UVA, Driver coached at William and Mary, UVA, and South Carolina. *Virginia Sports Hall of Fame 1988.*

- **FANNY CRENSHAW.** As a coach at Westhampton College, Fanny served on the school's staff for more than 40 years. A gifted athlete in archery and swimming, the Richmond native was the founder of the Virginia Field Hockey Association. *Virginia Sports Hall of Fame 1988.*

- **RAYMOND BUSSARD.** A native of Highland County, Ray was a nationally recognized track and field star at Bridgewater College in the 1950s. After graduation, he began a legendary coaching career and accumulated more than 800 victories at the high school and college level in a variety of sports. *Virginia Sports Hall of Fame 2000.*

VIRGINIA SPORTS HALL OF FAME NOTABLES
Additional "Champions of the Commonwealth" Inductees

- **WILLIAM "PAPPY" GOOCH.** A star quarterback at UVA, Pappy later served as a successful and popular coach at William and Mary. *Virginia Sports Hall of Fame 1986.*

- **HENRY HUCLES.** Henry coached Virginia Union's "The Dream Team" from 1939 to 1943 and led his cagers to four straight CIAA championships. He also served as a successful head gridiron coach for the Panthers from 1919 through 1942 and posted a record of 114-53-23. *Virginia Sport Hall of Fame 1997.*

- **LOUIS "WEENIE" MILLER.** A native of Richmond, Weenie Miller excelled on the gridiron at Benedictine High and the University of Richmond, where he earned All-State and All-Conferences honors. After his playing days, he coached a variety of sports teams at Glen Allen High, the University of Richmond, Hampden-Sydney College, Washington and Lee, and VMI. *Virginia Sports Hall of Fame 1994.*

- **RICHARD SMITH.** A coaching legend at Washington and Lee for 30 years, Richard served as the athletic director from 1921 to 1954. *Virginia Sports Hall of Fame 1976.*

- **LEIGH WILLIAMS.** A talented multi-sport star at Washington and Lee, Leigh earned 16 letters from 1927 to 1932 in football, basketball, baseball, and track. He once held the state record in the 440-yard dash. *Virginia Sports Hall of Fame 1974.*

- **PENELOPE MCBRIDE.** A winner of numerous state and mid-Atlantic tennis tournaments, Penelope was a member of the 1928 Wightman Cup squad and quarter finalist in the U.S. Nationals five times in her career. *Virginia Sports Hall of Fame 1983.*

- **RICHARD ALPHONSO SMITH.** In 1924, Alphonso and his playing partner Eddie Jacobs captured the Boys National Doubles Title. In a strange twist of fate, the same duo re-teamed 55 years later and won the National Seniors Doubles Championship. A formidable player on the senior circuit, Alphonso won 30 national championships over his playing career. *Virginia Sports Hall of Fame 1976.*

- **LOU PLUMMER.** A track and field legend at William and Mary, Lou began his coaching career at the prep level and assumed many of the coaching duties at the Norfolk Division of William and Mary from 1956 to 1974. *Virginia Sports Hall of Fame 1994.*

- **HARRISON FLIPPIN.** This gifted athlete won the National Pentathlon Championship in 1927 and once held the record for the 60-yard indoor high hurdles. As a physician, he served as medical director of the NFL. *Virginia Sports Hall of Fame 1975.*

- **WILLIAM "PETE" BENNETT.** A talented multi-sport athlete at Virginia State College in the early 1940s, Pete was named All-State in football and track and later served as coach at his alma mater. *Virginia Sports Hall of Fame 2002.*

PORTSMOUTH'S MAN AT THE MICROPHONE, MARTY BRENNAMAN. A native of Portsmouth, Marty Brennaman has forged a reputation in the sports broadcasting arena that is unsurpassed. In 1970, his voice was first heard throughout the Hampton Roads area on WTAR as he described the ABA action of the Virginia Squires and did play-by-play commentary for the Tidewater Tides. During the early 1970s, Marty was awarded Virginia Sportscaster of the Year four straight years. In 1974, he was chosen over 200 applicants to fill the shoes of Al Michaels in the Cincinnati Reds broadcast booth. For more than 30 years, Marty has provided a colorful, concise, and intelligent interpretation of the game. In 2000, Marty Brennaman entered the National Baseball Hall of Fame as the recipient of the Ford C. Frick Award. *Virginia Sports Hall of Fame 1999.*

SIX
Masters of the Media

Within the community of sports, the unsung heroes of the game are the individuals who take the time to promote athletics with a computer, typewriter, microphone, or television camera rather than a ball, bat, racquet, or iron. The impact of the media on sports has been enormous, and the everyday fan comes to expect their daily fix of news to include a healthy and generous portion of the latest events on the athletic fields locally, nationally, and even internationally. Without the many men and women who bring this information to the fan, the game would be enjoyed by only the very few who have the opportunity to see the event firsthand. Much is learned as one dissects the box scores or peruses the daily column in the local paper for a critique of the game. Without the media, the excitement and intricacies of sports would be limited and much less debated. Therefore, this chapter honors the inductees of the Virginia Sports Hall of Fame who made names for themselves on the airwaves or in daily print as they covered the games.

Two inductees of the Virginia Sports Hall of Fame are also members of the National Baseball Hall of Fame in Cooperstown: Marty Brennaman and Herb Carneal. Marty is a native of Portsmouth, Virginia, and honed his play-by-play skills in rural North Carolina. He returned to Hampton Roads to become "The Voice of the Virginia Squires" of the American Basketball Association. In the off-season, he provided area listeners with exciting play-by-play analysis of Tidewater Tides games. After only four years at the minor league level, Marty became a part of the "Big Red Machine" and began a long and respected career in the broadcasting booth for the National League Cincinnati Reds. Marty's counterpart in Cooperstown, Herb Carneal, served as the dual voice for the Philadelphia Athletics and Phillies before he relocated to Minnesota in 1962 to cover the Twins. Both of these unique and talented sports analysts provided countless baseball memories to generations of fans. Another respected and admired announcer native to the commonwealth is Frank Messer. While not a member of Cooperstown's elite, Frank has served as the calm and knowledgeable voice of the Baltimore Orioles and, later, the New York Yankees.

The print media is well represented in this chapter, with several Hampton Roads reporters honored in the Virginia Sports Hall of Fame, including veteran sportswriters Abe Goldblatt, George McClelland, Bob Moskowitz, Charles Karmosky, and Bill Leffler. Each of these wordsmiths presented the news of local baseball, football, and basketball events to their readers with utmost accuracy and sharp-witted flair.

The Richmond area is represented with such legendary reporters as Laurence Leonard, Chauncey Durden, Jennings Culley, Bill Deekens, Jerry Linquist, Marshall Johnson, and Bill Millsaps, as well as announcer Frank Soden. Northern Virginia is represented by Eddie Crane, while the Roanoke area can claim Bob McLelland. Both of these respected reporters made a name for themselves on the pages of their local papers and spread the word of sports events to their devoted readers in a unique manner.

Each and every one of these unsung heroes advanced sports in Virginia to a higher level because of their skill with the microphone or keyboard. Without their commentary, fans of Virginia sports would have missed an integral part of the game.

BILL LEFFLER, A MAN OF MANY WORDS. A native of Alabama, Bill Leffler began his career as a cub reporter for the *Portsmouth Star*. By 1957, Bill moved on to Norfolk's *Virginian-Pilot* and remained in their sports department until his retirement in 1996. For more than 41 years, no other reporter in the history of the *Pilot* or the *Ledger-Star* wrote more by-line stories than Bill Leffler. His contributions went beyond the sports pages of the local paper, as he was a leader in the creation of many youth sports programs in Portsmouth. In 1987, the Portsmouth Sports Club named Bill their Sportsman of the Year. *Virginia Sports Hall of Fame 2003.*

SPORTS EDITOR LAURENCE LEONARD. An icon in the Richmond papers for years, Laurence Leonard began his career as a reporter for the *Greensboro Daily News* and worked his way up to become sports editor by the late 1930s. In 1947, he arrived on the Richmond scene and accepted a position in the sports department of the *Times-Dispatch*. After a stint in the military as a reporter for the *Stars and Stripes*, Laurence served as sports information officer at William and Mary and was later selected as the sports editor for the *Richmond News Leader. Virginia Sports Hall of Fame 1997.*

GEORGE MCCLELLAND. A native of New Jersey, George arrived in Norfolk, took a position as a sports editor with the *Virginian-Pilot* in 1955, and headed the sports department until his retirement in 1987. During that time, readers found his daily column filled with interesting and controversial sports-related stories. In his final year with the *Pilot*, George was named Virginia's Sports Writer of the Year. After he turned in his typewriter in 1987, he fulfilled a lifelong dream and served as general manager and consultant for the St. Lucie Mets. *Virginia Sports Hall of Fame 2001.*

BROADCASTER FRANK SODEN. While not a native of Virginia, Frank is widely recognized as one of the most versatile voices on the airwaves throughout commonwealth. Early in his career, he provided the play-by-play for the Richmond Virginians and later the Braves. When not plying his trade at the ballpark, Frank found time to call University of Virginia, Virginia Tech, and University of Richmond football contests. From 1950 to 1975, Frank served as commentator for numerous NCAA and Southern Conference basketball contests. *Virginia Sports Hall of Fame 1998.*

SPORTS REPORTER ABE GOLDBLATT. From his early days as a school reporter at Portsmouth's Wilson High to his final story in the early 1990s, Abe covered the local pro, prep, and collegiate sporting events throughout the Hampton Roads area for the *Virginian-Pilot*. *Virginia Sports Hall of Fame 1997.*

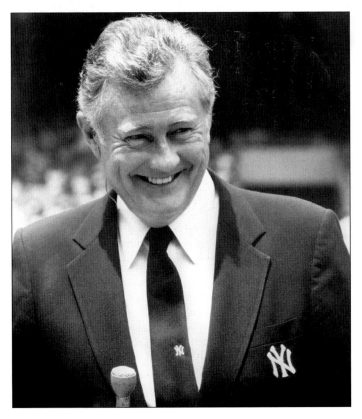

FRANK MESSER. Early in his career, Frank broadcast Richmond Virginian games and served as WRNL's sports director. From 1954 to 1962, he was named Virginia Sportscaster of the Year three times. Frank later accepted a job in the broadcast booth in Baltimore, which led to a position behind the mike with the New York Yankees and the NBA Knicks. Frank eventually covered numerous World Series and Super Bowl contests on both radio and television. *Virginia Sports Hall of Fame 2001.*

HERB CARNEAL, THE LEGENDARY VOICE OF THE MINNESOTA TWINS. A native of Richmond, Herb Carneal graduated from John Marshall High and accepted a broadcasting position with local station WMBG. After doing play-by-play in a number of minor league cities, his first major league job was to cover both the Athletics and Phillies for Philadelphia stations WFIL and WIBG. In 1962, Herb was hired by the Minnesota Twins and remained with the organization for over 40 years. In 1996, Herb was inducted into baseball's Hall of Fame and was awarded the Ford C. Frick Award. *Virginia Sports Hall of Fame 2002.*

CHAUNCEY DURDEN, 50 YEARS BEHIND THE TYPEWRITER. From 1936 until his last column in 1986, Chauncey covered horseracing, baseball, college football, and a myriad of sporting events from his desk at the *Richmond Times-Dispatch*. He was instrumental in bringing International League baseball to Richmond in 1954. *Virginia Sports Hall of Fame 1997.*

SPORTSWRITER STEVE GUBACK. For 30 years, Steve Guback served the Richmond and Washington areas with his coverage of landmark sporting events. At the *Washington Star*, he covered the Redskins for 12 years and served on special projects for the team when the *Star* ceased operations in 1981. Steve was voted the Virginia/District of Columbia Sportswriter of the Year three times and served as director of information for the President's Council on Physical Fitness and Sports. He was inducted into the Basketball Writers Hall of Fame in 1989. *Virginia Sports Hall of Fame 2005.*

VIRGINIA SPORTS HALL OF FAME NOTABLES
Additional "Masters of the Media" Inductees

◆ **BILL BRILL.** Born in Philadelphia and raised in Middlesex County, Virginia, Bill commenced his illustrious newspaper career as a fledgling sports writer for the *Covington Virginian* in 1952. By 1956, he joined the *Roanoke Times* as a staff reporter and within four years was promoted to sports editor. Bill was named Virginia Sportswriter of the Year in 1991. *Virginia Sports Hall of Fame 1999.*

◆ **EDDIE CRANE.** A gifted sports reporter and editor for the *Alexandria Gazette* and later the *Washington Star*, Eddie was honored with the Virginia Sportswriters Association Member Award in 1969. *Virginia Sports Hall of Fame 2000.*

◆ **JENNINGS CULLEY.** A longtime sports writer, columnist, and editor at the *Richmond News Leader* for more than 40 years, Jennings was named Virginia Sportswriter of the Year twice during an illustrious print career. *Virginia Sports Hall of Fame 1998.*

◆ **BILL DEEKENS.** A graduate of UVA and Columbia, Bill's prolific career as a sportswriter began in 1948 with the *Richmond News Leader*. In 1964, Bill was named Virginia Sportswriter of the Year. *Virginia Sports Hall of Fame 2002.*

◆ **CHARLES KARMOSKY.** A respected sports editor at the *Daily Press* from 1948 until his retirement in 1983, Charles was instrumental in the construction of historic War Memorial Stadium and Hampton Coliseum. *Virginia Sports Hall of Fame 1997.*

◆ **JERRY LINQUIST.** A legendary sports reporter for the *Richmond Times-Dispatch*, Jerry was one of the first to cover NASCAR locally and provided excellent coverage of the Richmond Braves and the Richmond Robins. He has been honored with numerous Virginia Press Association awards and was named AHL Hockey Writer of the Year. *Virginia Sports Hall of Fame 2003.*

◆ **BOB McLELLAND.** Born in Roanoke, Bob was a gifted sports writer and editor for the *Roanoke Times & World News* from 1949 to 1980. Away from the typewriter, he coached community football teams for 45 years. *Virginia Sports Hall of Fame 1998.*

◆ **MARSHALL JOHNSON.** This gifted writer began an illustrious newspaper career at the *Lynchburg News* and the *Manassas Journal* and developed into a respected reporter and sports editor for the Associated Press. *Virginia Sports Hall of Fame 1997.*

◆ **BILL MILLSAPS.** A respected sports writer throughout the commonwealth, Bill joined the *Richmond Times-Dispatch* in 1966 and became an executive editor in 1994. He was named Virginia Sportswriter of the Year 11 times over his career. *Virginia Sports Hall of Fame 2000.*

◆ **BOB MOSKOWITZ.** A native of New York City, Bob put together a writing career that spanned more than 50 years, with the majority of his time spent behind the typewriter at the *Daily Press*. *Virginia Sports Hall of Fame 2004.*

ABOUT THE AUTHOR

With this, his third published book, author Clay Shampoe continues a journey to research and chronicle Virginia's rich sports history. The author's previous works, *Baseball In Norfolk, Virginia* and *Baseball In Portsmouth, Virginia*, both published by Arcadia, showcase the area's baseball legends. Clay is a speech-language pathologist at Children's Hospital of The King's Daughters in Norfolk and is a longtime member of the Society for American Baseball Research (SABR). He currently resides in the Sandbridge area of Virginia Beach with his wife, Deborah. Future books are planned to recount the history of the Tidewater Tides and retell the rise and fall of the Virginia Squires. Clay is shown during a research visit to the National Baseball Hall of Fame in Cooperstown. (Photo by Jim Shampoe.)

VIRGINIA SPORTS HALL OF FAME INFORMATION

- ◆ Address: Virginia Sports Hall of Fame and Museum
             206 High Street
             Portsmouth, Virginia 23704

- ◆ Phone: 757-393-8031

- ◆ Email: info@vshfm.com

- ◆ Website: www.vshfm.com